The Educational Assistant's Guide to
# Supporting Inclusion
# in a Diverse Society

The Educational Assistant's Guide to
# Supporting Inclusion in a Diverse Society

CAROLE MASSING

BONNIE ANDERSON

CAROL ANDERSON

Brush
Education Inc.

20 21 22 23 24 5 4 3 2 1

Printed and manufactured in Canada

Brush Education Inc.

www.brusheducation.ca

contact@brusheducation.ca


Cover and interior design: Carol Dragich, Dragich Design

Cover images: iStock: 525962825/jarenwicklund; iStock : 828808382/FatCamera; iStock:1187260341/kali9; iStock:1124231378/Lidiia Moor

Editing: Kay Rollans


**Library and Archives Canada Cataloguing in Publication**

Title: The educational assistant's guide to supporting inclusion in a diverse society / Carole Massing, Bonnie Anderson, Carol Anderson.

Names: Massing, Carole, 1946- author. | Anderson, Bonnie, 1958- author. | Anderson, Carol, 1953- author.

Description: Includes bibliographical references.

Identifiers: Canadiana (print) 2020025457X | Canadiana (ebook) 2020025488X | ISBN 9781550598582 (softcover) | ISBN 9781550598599 (PDF) | ISBN 9781550598605 (Kindle) | ISBN 9781550598612 (EPUB)

Subjects: LCSH: Multicultural education—Canada. | LCSH: Learning—Social aspects—Canada. | LCSH: Teachers' assistants—Training of—Canada.

Classification: LCC LC1099.5.C3 M37 2020 | DDC 370.1170971—dc23

We acknowledge the support of the Government of Canada
Nous reconnaissons l'appui du gouvernement du Canada | Canadä

# Table of Contents

# Acknowledgements

This book has grown from our deep commitment to creating learning environments where every student feels they belong: places where they can achieve and contribute. Finding ways to truly honour and celebrate the diversity that students bring to our classrooms has challenged us to constantly explore, develop, and advocate for inclusive practices. We are pleased to have this opportunity to share what we have learned and to thank the students, colleagues, and families who have been a part of our journey. We are especially grateful to the educational assistants and teachers who have generously contributed their insights and experiences in hopes of creating a resource that will be useful to both new and practicing educational assistants.

Finally, we would like to express our appreciation to our families and friends for their enthusiasm and support. We would particularly like to thank Carlos Salegio for creating the graphics and Mary Lynne Matheson for sharing her knowledge and materials about child guidance strategies.

# Introduction

As Canadians, we take pride in the diversity of our society. We acknowledge our responsibilities to the Indigenous Peoples on whose traditional lands we live. We have enshrined in law the equal rights of individuals regardless of ethnicity, race, religion, language, gender identity, sex, sexual orientation, or ability. We declare that diversity is our strength; that it brings many different perspectives and abilities to the task of nation building. However, we are often reminded of the complexity and the challenge of melding such a diverse array of beliefs, attitudes, and realities into one cohesive and well-functioning whole.

Schools have the responsibility of preparing individuals to be productive members of society, helping them develop the knowledge, skills, attitudes, and abilities to contribute to an inclusive society. This is an important but complicated and demanding task.

Consider the classroom described below. It's a typical twenty-first century Canadian classroom with 26 students in total. Notice the different kinds of diversity that are found in this class. What challenges and opportunities do they present with respect to fostering learning and building respect for diversity?

> Of the 26 students in the class, two are recent refugees, three came to Canada as immigrants, while three others are the children of immigrants. Three of these children have a solid foundation in their first language but very little English.
> The two children who were refugees had had little formal schooling.
>
> The students in the class all come from various family constellations. Two have divorced parents who are both still very involved with their children. Two others come from a lone

parent family; one of these is a family with six children. One child lives with her two mothers. Another lives with a father who is transitioning from male to female. Another child lives with his grandmother because his mother struggles with mental health issues. The father of another child is rumoured to be dealing drugs.

Several of the families experience food scarcity. They rely heavily on the Food Bank and on the breakfasts the school provides for their children. Some students spend a lot of time on social media because their parents are very busy working to provide for their family.

One child has been diagnosed with autism. Another has violent outbursts during which the other children in the class are taken out of the classroom in order to stay safe.

While there are obviously a number of challenges in this classroom, there are at least as many strengths.

One child loves baseball and can tell you the World Series winners for the last 40 years. Another fills their notebook with long, detailed stories about fantastical creatures. Another child is noted for their kindness to classmates, and yet another is a skilled gymnast and aspires to someday compete on the national team.

An Indigenous child is happy to share some of the traditional knowledge they learned from their kookum with other students, and the family of a Jewish student has offered to explain Hanukkah traditions to the class.

There is a child who is a gifted mathematician. There is another who paints their feelings in vibrant colours during art class. Two of the children from families new to Canada are emerging into the world of English and eager to participate in the recess soccer games. There is the child who takes care of younger siblings while their mom cleans offices at night and the one who looks after their grandmother when she is ill.

The children in this typical classroom are learning valuable lessons from being immersed in a microcosm of Canadian society. Individually and collectively they have much to offer one another in terms of knowledge, skills, and support. If their teacher, with the help of the educational assistant, can bring them together into a cohesive and caring community, they will have a successful year.

---

This book is intended to help you, as an educational assistant (EA), build the skills you need to help create a community of learners where every child feels they belong, are valued, and can develop to their full potential.

Each of the 14 chapters in this book will focus on a foundational skill that is essential to your success as an EA. Every chapter includes certain elements intended to help direct your learning, study, and reflection. The "Learning Objectives" included at the beginning of each chapter will prepare you for the information ahead, and signal important points to keep in mind as you work through the material. A list of "Takeaways" at the end of every chapter can be used to review key points and test the information you've retained. "Discussion and Reflection" questions conclude each chapter; these questions are meant to help you broaden and deepen your learning with your classmates.

Chapter 1 takes a closer look at the diversity of Canadian society by elaborating on some of the subgroups that exist within it and their implications for schools. You will be encouraged to reflect on what these complexities mean for you as an EA.

As explained in Chapter 2, students with exceptionalities—that is, children who have physical, intellectual, or behavioural challenges—are an important part of Canada's societal diversity. As an EA, you will often be assigned to work with these students. Chapter 2 explores changing attitudes about the education of children with exceptionalities and looks at the intent and characteristics of inclusive education.

Chapter 3 outlines your role and responsibilities as an EA, including the attitudes and behaviours that will allow you to demonstrate your professionalism. This chapter addresses the importance of becoming familiar with policies and procedures at your school, and outlines a typical protocol for responding to an intruder in the school.

Chapter 4 looks at the EA's role as an advocate. As an EA, you will act as an advocate for students and help them learn to advocate for themselves. This advocacy role could involve working with the teacher to find appropriate resources to assist students and their families. It could also involve responding to disclosures or suspicions of abuse or neglect. This chapter also looks at ways to be effective in advocating for yourself and your profession.

In Chapter 5 you will learn about the value of developing a reflective practice as tools for learning. This chapter includes a structured process for working through puzzling situations as well as an exercise to help you become aware of biases that might stand in the way of your learning and relationships.

The work of an EA is a practice of relationships. You will spend much of your day interacting with students, teachers, families, and other team members. Chapter 6 explores the possible structure and dynamics of those relationships, while Chapter 7 looks at communication: a critical skill in all relationships.

Brain research, investigations of resiliency, theories of intelligence and self-esteem all indicate the importance of an approach to learning that takes into account the whole range of human needs and abilities. Chapter 8 briefly summarizes research and theory about the kinds of environment and support that children need to facilitate their healthy development.

Chapter 9 introduces you to the concept of universal design for learning (UDL) and strategies for differentiating learning in classrooms. Chapter 10 goes on to discuss supports for differentiating learning in academic subjects, while Chapter 11 addresses supports for developing students' social skills.

As an EA, you will work with many students who have behaviours that are challenging. Chapter 12 will show you how to respond to difficult behaviours in ways that are respectful to students and help them learn skills for self-regulation.

Your observations of children will guide both your interactions with them and the decisions that direct how you work with them. They will also provide valuable information to the teacher and other team members. In Chapter 13, you will learn about many different kinds of observation that allow you to collect and use relevant information about the children in your classroom.

The work you do as an EA is tremendously important but can also be stressful and exhausting. For that reason, Chapter 14 is about looking after yourself by maintaining the resources of mind, body, and spirit that enable you to be a source of inspiration to others.

As an EA, you have the opportunity to make a profound difference in the lives of students. You are also helping to shape a society that values and uses the strengths of diversity. We hope that this book will help you feel comfortable as you move into this role. We hope, too, that it will be a resource that you revisit from time to time during your working career, and that it will act as a reminder that you are doing a good and important job.

# Notes on Terminology

In this book, we have frequently used the abbreviation *EA* in place of the term *educational assistant*.

The term *family* refers to persons who are primarily responsible for a child. This may include the child's parents, guardians, or members of their extended family. The term *family* or *families* is, therefore, used throughout the book except in cases where it is clear that only *parent* applies.

The term *educator* is sometimes used and may refer to either an EA or a teacher. Gender-neutral language is used wherever possible; for example, "A child ties *their* shoes" refers to the shoes of that particular child.

The term *environment* refers to the circumstances or conditions surrounding a child or an activity. It may refer to a classroom, school, home, or the broader community in which a child lives.

# Our Diverse Society

*We are all different, which is great because we are all
unique. Without diversity life would be very boring.*

—CATHERINE PULSIFER

## Learning Outcomes

This chapter discusses multiculturalism in Canada and some of the groups that
make up our diverse population. After you have read this chapter, you will be
able to answer these questions:

- Why is multiculturalism an important part of Canada's national identity?
- What are some types of diversity that exist in our society?
- How would you describe yourself in relation to some of these types of
  diversity?
- Why is it particularly important to know about the history of Indigenous
  Peoples in Canada?
- What are some of the implications for the educational system that arise
  from various types of diversity we see in the classroom?
- What is your role as an EA in supporting inclusion in classrooms and schools?

## Introduction

At the beginning of this book, you were introduced to a typical twenty-first
century Canadian classroom. The children in this classroom represent various cultures, languages, family compositions, religions, lifestyles, abilities,
and socioeconomic backgrounds. They also—and it is important to always
remember this—bring wonderful strengths that aren't related to any of
these characteristics. It is these strengths that make the classroom a vibrant,

caring, and thriving community. This is the environment that you, as an EA, will help to nourish.

It is important that you understand the roots of Canada's commitment to multiculturalism and diversity. As well, you must have a good awareness of the particular challenges and opportunities certain groups face within our educational system. With this background knowledge you, the EA, will be able to understand and respond appropriately to the diverse needs of the children where you work.

## Canada's Commitment to Multiculturalism

Canada's commitment to equity and diversity is framed by the Canadian Multicultural Act. This Act builds upon the Canadian Charter of Rights and Freedoms, which forms the first part of the Constitution Act (1982). Enacted in 1988, the Canadian Multicultural Act begins with a statement that "multiculturalism reflects the cultural and racial diversity of Canadian society and acknowledges the freedom of all members of Canadian society to preserve, enhance and share their cultural heritage" (§3.1.a). It ensures that every person has equal rights under the law and "has the freedom of conscience, religion, thought, belief, opinion, expression, peaceful assembly and association and guarantees those rights and freedoms equally to male and female persons" (preamble). Although not without problems and challenges, Canada's commitment to multiculturalism is seen as unique, largely successful, and a defining part of Canada's national identity.

## What Is Diversity?

What do we mean by *diversity*? The Government of Ontario (2009) has defined diversity as "[t]he presence of a wide range of human qualities and attributes within a group, organization, or society. The dimensions of diversity include, but are not limited to, ancestry, culture, ethnicity, gender, gender identity, language, physical and intellectual ability, race, religion, sex, sexual orientation, and socio-economic status" (p. 4).

It's important to recognize that we are all a part of this diversity, and all occupy positions along the spectrum of each of these dimensions of diversity. These characteristics can help you to define the self that you bring to society and to your work with children.

## Our Diverse Origins

In this section, we'll look at three important groups that exist in our diverse society: Indigenous Peoples, immigrants, and refugees. We will consider some of the unique histories and life situations that children who belong to these groups bring into the classroom.

## Indigenous Children and Families

The term *Indigenous* is used to describe the First Nations, Inuit, and Métis Peoples. Indigenous Peoples have inhabited the land we now call Canada for thousands of years, beginning, by some estimates, approximately 11,000 years before the arrival of European settlers (Stonechild, 2006).

Contact with English and French settlers and with colonial regimes significantly disrupted the lives of Indigenous people. The main aim of colonial policies was to "clear the plains" (Daschuk, 2013) of Indigenous people to make way for agricultural and industrial development. Epidemics and the depletion of buffalo herds caused mass starvation and death (Daschuk, 2013). Canada signed treaties with many Indigenous nations (with the notable exception of those in areas of British Columbia and the North). Canada's interpretation of these treaties led to the cession of traditional lands to the Crown and the establishment of reserves that often were not located in desirable places.

Colonial policies and missionary activities sought to further destroy traditional Indigenous cultures in order to assimilate Indigenous Peoples into the cultural mainstream.

The Truth and Reconciliation Commission Report of 2015 brought to the attention of the general public the injustices that colonialism perpetrates upon Indigenous Peoples in Canada. In particular, it brought into the open the devastating effects of Canada's residential school system, which was designed to erase Indigenous languages and cultures, and destroy children's connections to their families (TRC, 2015; Fine, 2015). Indigenous Peoples today are reclaiming their identity, but do so in the face of continuing intergenerational trauma (Hackett, Feeny & Tompa, 2016), structural inequities (Beedie, Macdonald & Wilson, 2019), and racism (Government of Canada, 2019).

As of 2016, there were 1.7 million Indigenous people in Canada, comprising 4.9% of the population (Block, 2017). Indigenous children are more

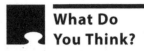

## What Do You Think?

How you would describe yourself with respect to each of the dimensions of diversity mentioned above?

- Ancestry
- Culture
- Ethnicity
- Gender identity
- Language
- Physical ability
- Intellectual ability
- Race
- Religion
- Socioeconomics

likely than non-Indigenous children to be living in poverty. Given the historical legacy of the residential schools and current fears of child welfare apprehension, it is understandable that some Indigenous families might feel mistrustful of non-Indigenous school personnel.

Indigenous children and families need to be able to "see" themselves in classrooms and feel that they belong. EAs and teachers who are Indigenous are important resources because they are seen to be understanding of the life circumstances and experiences of Indigenous families (Kemble, 2019) and also because they can suggest meaningful and authentic ways to represent Indigenous knowledge in curricula and in school structures (Stagg-Peterson, Huston & Loon, 2018). Changing the focus of the school curriculum to reinforce the culture and values of each child's family is seen as important, as is encouraging the preservation of Indigenous languages (McCue, 2018).

Research has suggested, however, that simply paying extra attention to Indigenous culture in class is not sufficient to help Indigenous students feel, and be, fully included. Educators need to be aware of, and address, their unconscious biases, which may result in lowered expectations for Indigenous children. Furthermore, Non-Indigenous students may not understand, and may therefore resent, a heavy focus on Indigenous cultures. Even the introduction of cultural activities into the classroom can be alienating for Indigenous students. If an educator introduces an Indigenous cultural activity that isn't part of the culture to which the Indigenous student belongs, it may place the student in a position where they are expected to be an expert on something they know nothing about. It could also create a situation in which non-Indigenous peers think they understand an Indigenous student's culture but really don't (Gebhard, 2018).

It's important to be aware of both the history of the Indigenous Peoples of Canada and the present challenges they face. Indigenous students are often subject to stereotypes, racial slurs, and discrimination, making it important that schools overtly address issues of bias and racism (Gebhard, 2018) and that educators reflect on their own preconceptions and biases in order to avoid passing them along in school. The strength and resilience of Indigenous Peoples have allowed them to survive the ongoing history of colonialism in Canada, and are the foundation for the work that many Indigenous communities are doing to reclaim their inherent rights and their traditional languages and cultures. Recognizing and supporting the strengths and aspirations of Indigenous students in your classroom will support this important work.

## Newcomers to Canada

Immigrants and refugees form a sizable and ever-increasing proportion of Canada's population. Statistics Canada estimates that by 2036, immigrants born outside Canada will comprise between 24.5% and 30% of the population (Morency, Malenfont, & MacIsaac, 2017). If we add second-generation immigrants (individuals with at least one parent born abroad), that number will increase to almost half the population. Many Canadians are fond of citing our multicultural "quilt" or "mosaic" as evidence of our superiority over American society's dream of cultural assimilation (the cultural "melting pot"). However, many would agree that there are cracks in this mosaic.

Newcomers are inevitably faced with challenges: culture shock, language barriers, loss of extended family support, loneliness, navigating unfamiliar systems, discrimination, and adjusting to the climate, to name a few. Lack of recognition of credentials from their home countries often results in unemployment or underemployment. Families may also experience role reversals. In some, the children may become the "experts" of the new culture more quickly than the parents do. In others, husbands may have to adjust to losing their traditional role as the breadwinners of their families. The stress associated with these challenges may influence family members' emotional and physical wellbeing.

These are issues that many immigrants face even though they have moved voluntarily and have had an opportunity to plan for their move. Refugees, however, have been forced to leave their home country because of war, persecution, or natural disasters. They may have ongoing challenges arising from their premigration, migration, and settlement experiences. Many, including children and young people, have witnessed violence or been direct victims of torture and abuse. Usually refugees have come to Canada by way of one or more other (asylum) countries, and the conditions in those countries have often been very difficult. Once they are settled in Canada, they face all of the challenges of finding their way in a new environment, along with the effects of the trauma they have experienced in their journey to Canada.

Families who arrive as refugees may not know, as they leave their home country, what their final destination will be, and have had little time to prepare for life in their new country. Their children arrive with varying educational backgrounds and often without the language of their new school. The trauma they have suffered may manifest itself in symptoms that will affect them in school, such as disturbed sleep, difficulty concentrating, anxiety, anger, or hopelessness (Jesuit Social Services, 2009).

School staff will need to be sensitive to the trauma refugee children have experienced and the challenges they are facing. At the same time, it is important to remember that they are survivors, with strengths and resilience.

It is also important to remember that many immigrants and refugees come from countries with very different school systems. Families may not understand that they are welcome to participate and contribute at their children's school. In such cases, an explicit invitation can help confirm that their input is valued.

Many Canadians and organizations have welcomed newcomers with open arms. Unfortunately, others have reacted with fear and prejudice. Like Indigenous students, newcomer students are frequently subjected to racist comments and treatment. Educators and EAs must be observant, sensitive, and self-reflective in order to provide an inclusive environment for these vulnerable students.

## Diverse Religions and Languages

There are some opportunities in Canada for individuals to be educated according to religious and language preferences, such as in private schools or in language-specific or faith-based school districts. Still, it often falls to public systems to accommodate diverse religions and languages in ways that help all students feel respected and included.

### Religions

Canada has no official religion and the Charter of Rights and Freedoms supports freedom of religion. The 2011 Canadian census found that Christianity had the greatest number of adherents (67.3%). People with no religion represented 23.9% of the population. The remainder of the population was split among Islam (3.2%), Hinduism (1.5%), Sikhism (1.4%), Buddhism (1.1%), and Judaism (1.0%) (Statistics Canada, 2013).

There are some faith-based schools associated with specific religions. The most common are Christian and Catholic, but there are also Islamic, Jewish, Sikh, and Buddhist schools, among others. Some Catholic schools are funded by specially directed taxes, but most other faith-based schools are privately funded.

> A Syrian refugee family is one of many who have expressed dismay that their children's school included Christmas activities while omitting any reference to the holidays that were important to them. (Christine Massing, personal communication, February 13, 2020)

Public schools are charged with providing a secular, inclusive experi-ence to all children. Controversy has arisen around the celebration of religious holidays, particularly Christmas, in public schools (Friesen & Bascaramurty, 2011; Taylor, 2014). Schools have responded to this criticism in various ways. Some, perhaps under pressure from mainstream families, continue to focus on Christmas and other dominant holidays. Others have changed traditional Christmas programs to a more general holiday theme. A few acknowledge the whole range of holidays celebrated by all the chil-dren in the school.

## Languages

English and French are the official languages of Canada, although other languages are becoming more common. In 2016, 78.9% of Canadians had English or French as their mother tongue. This is down from 80.2% in 2011, and 82.4% in 2001. The 2016 census showed 22.9% of respondents reported speaking a language other than English or French at home, up from 21.3% in 2011 (Statistics Canada, 2017a).

Some children are still being told to speak only English in the classroom. There are, however, many social and academic benefits to maintaining and supporting students' language diversity.

Reviving the use of traditional languages is central to Indigenous Peoples' revitalization of their cultures. Programs that teach those lan-guages are becoming more common. Teachers and EAs who speak one or more Indigenous languages are valuable assets in supporting these revital-ization efforts.

In the case of newcomers, maintaining children's home languages can help provide them with a solid basis for learning the majority language of their new home. It can also help to preserve ties with immediate and extended family. In the words of one Somali mother, "I can't talk to my children in English about important things." EAs and teachers who can speak more than one language are especially valuable in classrooms with newcomers. They can both welcome children who speak those languages and build trust with them and their families. They can also expose all of the children they work with to the possibilities of speaking more than one language.

Families should be encouraged to support their children in maintaining their home language. There is now a great deal of research showing the cog-nitive advantages of bilingualism for children (e.g., Bialystok, 2011; Chin & Wigglesworth, 2007; Kovaacs & Mehler, 2009). Analysis of research about English language learners (ELLs) has shown that educational programs that systematically incorporate the use of ELL home languages result in levels of academic success—including achievement in literacy and other academic subjects—that are as high as and often higher than those of ELLs in English-only programs (Genesee & Lindholm-Leary, 2011).

Children who are learning to read in a second language are often able to transfer skills and knowledge from their first language. The best evidence of this comes from studies showing that students with strong reading skills in their home language also have strong reading skills in their second language.

In addition to the academic advantages that children derive from knowing their home language, it is also important to consider how it benefits family cohesion. One school principal told of a large family in which the parents didn't speak English and the younger children had never learned the home language. "They couldn't speak with their parents", he lamented. "What kind of family is that?" While this is a dramatic example—most often the rupture of relationships is between the child and their extended family members who live in another location—it does highlight the importance of language to key relationships.

In reality, teachers and EAs will often not speak a child's home language. In these cases, remember that children and families still always appreciate you trying to learn some words in their home language. They may also enjoy teaching you certain phrases in their language.

## Societal Issues

Current social issues that deserve awareness and attention include poverty and issues of gender identity. Each can severely affect the academic and social wellbeing of students.

### Poverty

Rates of poverty in Canada are difficult to determine because they depend on how poverty is being measured and who is being counted. It is similarly difficult to determine rates of homelessness. It is nonetheless recognized that the families of many children live in poverty or are homeless.

It is, however, well-established that child poverty rates are higher among Indigenous children (especially those living on reserves), children living in lone-parent (usually single-mother) families, and children in new immigrant families.

Women, on average, earn less than men and are more likely to be below the poverty line. Lone-mother families are the most impoverished of all household types in Canada: 21% of all lone mothers are low income compared to just 5.5% of married couples.

Research by the Canadian Teachers' Federation links lower income to lower school achievement, less participation in extracurricular activities, less readiness to learn, irregular school attendance, lower career aspirations, increased risk of illiteracy, and delayed cognitive development (2020). We should not interpret these findings to mean that families with low incomes are incapable of supporting their children's learning or that they don't care about their children's achievement. They may be working shifts or multiple jobs in order to support their family and have little time or energy to focus on their children's schooling.

Children who are homeless or living in poverty may come to school hungry, lacking sleep, or without appropriate clothing. These conditions, and the stress that accompanies them, make it difficult for them to learn.

Teachers stress that whatever measures are put in place to help children living with poverty—meal subsidies and field trips, for example—must be carried out in a way that doesn't stigmatize these children. They also mention the importance of building trusting relationships with the children's families. This way, the families won't hesitate to contact the school when they need help for their child.

## Diverse Sexual and Gender Identities

Recent decades have seen increasing attention to matters of gender and sexual orientation. An individual's *gender identity* refers to the way in which they define themselves in relation to the masculine and feminine norms of their culture. Many people identify as male or female, and this gender may or may not correspond with their biological sex or the gender they were assigned at birth. Others' gender identities fall somewhere between male and female, or may be outside of this binary altogether. *Sexual orientation* has to do with the sexes or genders to which a person is romantically attracted. It could be people of the same sex, the opposite sex, both, or neither.

Students may face challenges at school because of their sexual orientation and gender identity, or those of members of their family. In 2005, Canada became the fourth country in the world to legalize same-sex marriage. By 2016 there were 72,880 same-sex couples in Canada, one-third of whom were married. In 2016, about 12% of the same-sex couples had children living with them, compared with about half of opposite-sex couples (Statistics Canada, 2017b). Research has shown overwhelmingly that children of gay and lesbian couples are as well-adjusted as children with heterosexual parents (Cornell University, 2017). Unfortunately, some same-sex families face discrimination in their communities and their children may be teased or bullied.

Most children and youth who identify as LGBTQ2S+[1] will be happy and thrive during their adolescent years if they have accepting families and are in a safe and supportive school environment. These youth especially need safe places and supportive environments at school if they do not have them at home.

Schools can help LGBTQ2S+ children and families by creating a safe and supportive environment for all students: one that prohibits bullying, harassment, and violence. They can recognize and model acceptance of diverse family configurations and gender identities through, for example, the books that are read to children and the materials used for classes. Developing health curricula that acknowledge and normalize diverse sexual orientations and gender identities, and that talk about safe sex practices for diverse orientations and identities, is important. Gay-straight alliances—that is, school clubs that are open to youth of all sexual orientations and genders—are also helpful tools that help teach acceptance to all students and can be an invaluable support to youth who identify as LGBTQ2S+ (Airton, 2020).

## The EA's Role in Working with Diversity

Canada's diversity is rich and complex. This chapter focused on some diverse populations in Canada, and addressed some of the implications this diversity has on the country's educational systems. All children and families have needs, challenges, and strengths that need to be accommodated and nurtured in the school environment. Teachers do a great deal toward that goal, but EAs also have an essential role. They can be a teacher's eyes and ears, and can also be the adults who are most readily accessible to students when teachers are focusing on broader curriculum goals. They are usually the ones who will respond to a distressed child's disruptive behaviour or help a struggling child understand an assignment. They are often the first and primary persons to greet and work with immigrant and refugee children. Even if they are assigned to just one child, the EA can be a powerful force for inclusion for all of the children in a classroom.

EAs are often designated to work with children or youth who have *exceptionalities*—challenges or delays in their physical, intellectual, emotional, social, language, or behavioural development. Children need to belong, be

---

[1]  The term *LGBTQ2S+* is used by the Queer community to refer to a large group of diverse gender identities and sexual orientations. The term specifically refers to those who identify as lesbian, gay, bisexual, trans* (referring to transmen and transwomen, as well as gender identities other than male and female), queer, and two-spirit (a third-gender identity used by some Indigenous people); the "+" acknowledges that many other identities and orientations exist.

valued, and contribute to class and to society, and children with exceptionalities are no different. In fact, children with exceptionalities have a legislated right to equal education. In Chapter 2, we will consider how EAs can support children with exceptionalities and give them the best possible educational opportunities.

## Takeaways

- Canada's commitment to diversities is framed by the Canadian Multicultural Act of 1988 and the Charter of Rights and Freedoms.
- It is particularly important that we, as Canadians, understand the significance of the history and experiences of Indigenous Peoples in Canada.
- We are all part of Canada's diversity, but understanding the experiences of particular groups in society can help EAs work more effectively with students.

## Reflection and Discussion

- What might people mean when they say there is strength in diversity?
- Was there information in this chapter that surprised you or changed your ideas?
- Based on the information in this chapter, what implications do you see for your work as an EA with:
  - › Indigenous children and families?
  - › Newcomer families?
  - › Students who celebrate holidays other than those of the mainstream religion in your school?
  - › Students who are learning to speak English?
  - › Students living in poverty?
  - › Students who are in the process of resolving their sexual or gender identity?
  - › Students with exceptionalities?
- Why might it be important to learn about the experiences of the children and families with whom you work?

# Considering Inclusion

*In diversity there is beauty and there is strength.*

—*MAYA ANGELOU*

## Learning Outcomes

In this chapter, we will consider philosophies and practices in providing educational services for children with exceptionalities. After you have read this chapter, you will be able to answer these questions:

- How is inclusion in education related to inclusion in society?
- What is an exceptionality?
- How have views of exceptionality, and the education of children with exceptionalities, changed over time?
- What is inclusion?
- What are some barriers to inclusion?

## Introduction

In this book, we refer to children with diverse abilities, challenges, or delays in some aspect of their learning, whether it be physical, intellectual, emotional, social, linguistic, or behavioural, as children with *exceptionalities*, though in your work you may also hear the term *special needs*, or, sometimes, *dis/abilities*. Attitudes about the education of children with exceptionalities are changing to create classrooms and schools that welcome all children, regardless of their individual abilities and circumstances. This reflects a vision of an equitable society where all people are included and are treated fairly and respectfully. Inclusive education is a way of creating equity in classrooms and schools.

## A Story of Exceptionality and Inclusion

When children are obviously different from their peers, it can be hard to find a way for them to belong. An EA can play an essential role in helping a student integrate into a school setting and feel a sense of inclusion and belonging.

*Inclusion* is the process of overcoming the barriers that limit the presence, participation, and achievement of certain learners. Let's look at one story of success in an inclusive educational environment.

> Petra, a 10-year-old who has a spinal cord injury, has just moved to a new school and is getting to know her EA, Wilma. One day Wilma asks her how she is finding her new school. "I like it better here," she says. "Before I was that freak in the wheelchair sitting in the corner. Here I have friends." As if on cue, one of her classmates, Jody, asks Petra if she can push her wheelchair into the library.

Wilma, Petra's EA, has worked hard to create an environment where Petra feels like a part of the group. She has:

- Welcomed Petra and introduced her to the class.
- Invited and answered questions (and encouraged Petra to answer questions) about Petra's medical condition.
- Identified a few students who might be open to being and working with Petra and has asked them to help with various tasks.
- Modeled how to interact with Petra; for example, pushing her wheelchair.
- Avoided being a barrier between Petra and her classmates by standing back where possible. She wants Petra to gain independence and not be inhibited by her presence.
- Provided opportunities for Petra to demonstrate her strengths and talents to the class.
- Supported the teacher in planning small group activities so Petra can interact with classmates and get the help she needs to complete tasks.
- Worked to help other school staff establish a relationship with Petra. She has helped them to understand Petra's abilities, interests, and needs. She has emphasized that Petra really wants to interact with

other students and has shared some of the ways she is working to facilitate that.

Physical exceptionalities such as Petra's spinal cord injury in the story above make students eligible for extra support that can help them have a successful school experience. Physical exceptionalities are, however, just one of several categories of exceptionality that may qualify students for additional assistance.

## What Kinds of Exceptionalities Do We See?

Additional funding is often allotted to schools to provide extra support for students who have exceptionalities related to behaviour, communication, or intellectual or physical ability. It is common for students to exhibit a combination of one or more exceptionalities.

Here are some of the exceptionalities you may encounter in your work as an EA:

- English language learning
- Gifted or talented
- Physical disability
- Medical or chronic health needs
- Blindness / visual impairment
- Deafness / hearing loss[2]
- Communication disorders
- Autism spectrum disorder (ASD)
- Intellectual disability
- Behaviour exceptionalities
- Learning disabilities

Different jurisdictions may have different criteria for determining whether a child qualifies for support in any of these areas.

## The Rights of Children with Exceptionalities

In Petra's story at the beginning of this chapter, Petra's EA Wilma found many ways to help Petra feel welcome in the school, make friends, and be successful in her learning. Wilma's efforts to include Petra reflect societal changes in attitudes toward the rights of individuals with exceptionalities.

Whether or not a child is considered to have exceptionalities, they fall under the protection of the United Nations Convention on the Rights of the

---

[2] Many families of children who are Deaf (i.e., belonging to the Deaf community) consider deafness a difference, not an impairment. *Hearing impairment* may be seen as an offensive term.

Child. This Convention was ratified by the Canadian government in 1991 and states, in part:

> No child should be treated unfairly on any basis. Children should not be discriminated against based on their race, religion or abilities; what they think or say; the type of family they come from; where they live, what language they speak, what their parents do, what gender they identify with, what their culture is, whether they have a disability or whether they are rich or poor. (Government of Canada, Nov. 2017, Article 2)

The Convention specifies that the best interests of children is the main concern in making decisions that affect them and that, depending on their maturity, children have the right to participate in decisions affecting them.

In 2012, an influential ruling by the Supreme Court of Canada gave students with disabilities the right to receive the accommodation measures they need to access and benefit from the service of public education.

Education falls under provincial and territorial, not federal, jurisdiction in Canada. Typically, the provinces and territories provide access to schooling for children from the age of 5 or 6 years to the age of 18 to 21 years. Educational policies regarding the education of children with disabilities vary across provinces and school jurisdictions. There are differences in the criteria for eligibility, the services provided, and the resources that are made available. In most provinces, children with disabilities tend to be included in mainstream classrooms, with accommodations or modifications to ensure their success. These provisions for the education of children with exceptionalities reflect changing attitudes about disability rights and the strengths of diversity.

## Changing Views on Exceptionality

Different cultures view exceptionality differently, and their views influence the provisions that are made for children with exceptionalities. Depending on the culture, a child with exceptionalities might be a source of shame or of pride. A child who is a source of shame may be hidden away from the public and lack opportunities for education or a productive life.

Definitions of exceptionality may depend on cultural norms. For example, in cultures where direct eye contact is considered disrespectful, the limited ability to maintain eye contact that is characteristic of children with ASD might be considered appropriate behaviour, and not stand out as an exceptionality.

Societal views of differing abilities affect the extent to which children with exceptionalities are included in mainstream classrooms. In some societies, children with even mild exceptionalities are put in *special education* classes or schools for remediation and to prevent them from being teased by peers.

In Canadian society, attitudes toward diverse abilities have changed over the years, and with them approaches to educating children with diverse abilities. In the late nineteenth century to the mid-twentieth century, there were no community services for children with exceptionalities. Families of children with exceptionalities were often advised by doctors that keeping them at home would be too difficult, so they should take them to an institution where they would be kept safe.

It's shocking to us now to consider that in 1910, Dr. Helen MacMurchy, a Canadian doctor who was at the time considered a progressive figure in child and maternal health, championed segregated classes for "feeble-minded" children because she believed they would grow up to be unemployed, degenerate criminals who would produce children much like them. Dr. MacMurchy is now understood to have been a prominent eugenicist (Marsh, 2011). Eugenics is the belief, widespread at the time, that forced sterilizations of individuals deemed by those in power to be genetically inferior would improve society (Marsh, 2011). The practice is now widely condemned. Still, forced sterilizations are documented to have continued into the 1970s in Alberta and British Columbia. Undocumented instances of forced sterilization are alleged to be taking place even today, affecting Indigenous women in particular (Kirup, 2018).

After World War II, there was more emphasis on human rights. A movement began that advocated for better treatment of people with exceptionalities. Wolf Wolfensberger and colleagues (1972), who were very influential in this movement, demanded that people with exceptionalities be released from institutions where they were kept, and that these institutions be replaced with community-based services to support these people.

In the years since, there has been a dramatic shift in the way Canadian society thinks about and supports diverse abilities and people with exceptionalities. While there is still much work to be done, there is also much to celebrate. In terms of education, all provinces and territories in Canada now provide educational services to children with diverse needs.

In some cases, educational provisions for children with exceptionalities involve the full inclusion of these children in mainstream classrooms. In others, the children are placed in special classrooms and programs, effectively separating them from their mainstream peers.

# From Segregation to Inclusion

There has been a general movement away from segregation to more inclusive services for students with exceptionalities. One reason for this shift is philosophical, stemming from the belief that students will benefit from association with mainstream peers. Another is financial: segregated classes usually have a higher student-to-teacher ratio, making them more expensive to operate.

Both segregation and inclusion have advantages and disadvantages. In a segregated classroom, students have more individualized attention. Their teachers often have special training to support their particular exceptionalities, and students may form a cohesive group in their classroom. On the other hand, segregated classes limit the opportunities for interaction with mainstream students and may contribute to a situation where the students are labelled by their exceptionalities.

Inclusive education focuses on providing for the needs of all children within a regular classroom. In reality, many classrooms strive to meet the needs of children with exceptionalities by including them in mainstream classrooms for some of the day, but taking them out to work on specific skills for the rest of the day.

## What Does Inclusive Education Look Like?

*Inclusive education* means that all students can attend their local schools in age-appropriate classes and share a common learning environment. They receive the support they need to learn and to participate in all aspects of school life from their teachers, EAs, and other support staff. Their diverse needs are met in ways that are respectful, accepting, and supportive.

A system of inclusive education involves:

- All school personnel valuing and supporting diversity
- Valuing all children within classrooms and the wider school community
- Developing a culture of high expectations and success for all
- Identifying and supporting students' strengths
- Recognizing and responding to students' needs
- Removing barriers within learning environments
- Supporting and developing understanding of and skills for inclusion at personal, school, and system levels
- Collaborating at all levels of the system to support the success of learners

## Arguments for Inclusive Education

Proponents of inclusion cite research that supports the positive effects of inclusive education for all children (Mitchell, 2014; Mitchell, 2010).

Inclusion BC (n.d.) argues that every child in a classroom benefits from inclusive education because it allows them to:

- Develop individual strengths and gifts through high and appropriate expectations for each child
- Work on individual goals while participating in the life of the classroom with other students their own age
- Involve their families in their education and in the activities of their local schools
- Foster a school culture of respect and belonging through opportunities to learn about and accept individual differences, lessening the impact of harassment and bullying
- Develop friendships with a wide variety of other children, each with their own individual needs and abilities

## Barriers to Inclusive Education

Inclusion isn't easy. Consider some of these conditions that have to be met in order to build an inclusive environment:

- Teaching and learning strategies and curricula have to be designed to accommodate the needs of each individual child.
- Schools may require structural changes to make them accessible to all.
- Assessment practices have to be constructed to include diverse areas of strength.
- Teachers need to have sufficient support from EAs and administration to work with the complexity of an inclusive classroom.
- Teachers must be trained to respond to a wide range of student needs and interests.
- Schools need to be sufficiently financed to provide adequate EA support.
- Educators, children, and families have to genuinely believe that each person has value and a right to fulfill their potential; they have to get beyond stereotypes and misconceptions to see each individual in all of their strengths and vulnerabilities.

As Parekh (2018) reminds us, when we talk about including students in a school environment, we have to consider exactly what that environment into which we want to include them is. Can we ensure that the school environment, culture, and curriculum will support all children to experience feelings of worth, capability, and belonging? Perhaps the best way to think about inclusion is as an ongoing enterprise: one that we are constantly working to improve and refine. Our commitment to this work will force us to be responsive and innovative in ways that will benefit all students.

## Implications for EAs

As an EA, you will probably be working in an inclusive or *integrated* environment with students that have exceptionalities in the categories mentioned above. While the teacher will be responsible for planning the curriculum, you, as an EA, will have a great deal of responsibility and opportunity to make that curriculum and the coursework it entails accessible and useful to each child, and to help integrate each child effectively in the broader school environment.

Chapter 3 will tell you more about the work that you will do as an EA and how to be effective in that role.

 **Takeaways**

- Attitudes toward diverse abilities and services for children with exceptionalities have evolved over time.
- Rights to education have been enshrined in international and Canadian law.
- There has been a wide-reaching movement from segregation to inclusion in schools.
- Decisions about the best educational setting for individual children should consider the extent to which the environment they are entering allows them to feel worthy and capable and to have a sense of belonging.
- Inclusion isn't easy; we should consider it a work in progress. In the best situations, it benefits all the children in a classroom or school.
- EAs are an important asset for supporting diversity.

 **Reflection and Discussion**

- What experiences have you had with children who have exceptionalities?
- What challenges might you anticipate in working with any of the exceptionalities identified in this chapter?
- Do you feel that inclusion is desirable in every situation? Why or why not?

## 3

# The Role of the Educational Assistant

*Anyone who does anything to help
a child is a hero to me.*

*—FRED ROGERS*

### Learning Outcomes

After reading this chapter, you will be able to answer these questions:

- What is an Educational Assistant (EA)?
- What does an EA do?
- Who is the EA accountable to? Teachers
- As an EA, what are your ethical obligations?
- Why is it important to conduct yourself in a professional manner?
- Why is it important to know your school's policies and procedures?

## Introduction

The previous chapter focuses on the work that EAs do with children who have exceptionalities. However, as you will see in this chapter, the role of the EA is not at all limited to assisting children who have exceptionalities.

Imagine that you have applied for a job as an EA and have been invited to an interview. What do you need to know to be as knowledgeable as possible about the position before you attend the interview? Alternatively, perhaps you have accepted the interview but are still deciding whether you really want to work as an EA. The information in this chapter could help you understand the roles an EA may play, and help you answer some of these questions.

## What Is an Educational Assistant (EA)?

*Educational assistant* is one of several titles a school district may use to refer to its educational support staff. Depending on where you are from, where you plan to work, and the specifics of the position you apply for, you may run into other titles such as *teacher assistant, paraprofessional, special needs education assistant, teacher aide,* or *education assistant.* These terms are all used to describe similar kinds of positions. The key role of the EA is to support a teacher by working with individual students or groups of students. EAs work alongside and under the supervision of teachers in order to help students develop the skills to be successful in school and in the larger community.

Consider the following scenario, in which Francine, a 32-year-old mother of two children, is applying for a position as an EA.

Francine has just been called for an interview for employment as an EA. She has experience working with children in her own family and has also worked in childcare. Francine has an idea of what EAs do, but has very little idea about specific expectations employers might have for EAs they hire, or the specific professional standards for EAs in her school district or province.

**What Do You Think?**

Francine is trying to prepare for her interview. What kind of information does Francine need to know about the role of an EA? What questions should she ask herself in order to prepare for her interview?

### Where Do EAs Work?

In addition to working in school settings, EAs may be employed in early intervention programs, alternative educational settings (private schools, special schools), children's treatment centres, vocational services, life skills programs, English as an Additional Language (EAL) community programs, childcare centres, and other learning organizations. In schools, EAs are usually considered to be support staff.

### Who Do EAs Work With?

EAs are often assigned to work with one student who has exceptionalities with respect to their mental, emotional, or physical functioning. However, unless the student requires intensive one-on-one support throughout the day, the EA will support the teacher within the whole classroom or even work with teachers in several classrooms. The EA may work as part of an interdisciplinary team with various consultants. This team might include occupational, physical, or speech and language therapists; psychologists; social workers; community support workers; or audiologists. The EA will build relationships with families, the school administration, and various teachers and EAs.

## What Do EAs Do?

The EA's duties are varied, depending on the needs of the students, the help required by the teacher, and the skills the EA brings to the work. The EA's responsibilities might include the following, adapted from the Alberta Teachers' Association (2015) and the Ontario Network of International Professionals (2020):

- Helping students with lessons, under the direct supervision of the classroom teacher
- Working with students who may be visually impaired or hard of hearing, or who have physical, mental, or sensory exceptionalities
- Implementing individual learning plans
- Observing and documenting student behaviours, and making suggestions to the teacher based on those observations
- Accompanying and supervising students during activities outside the classroom
- Diffusing conflicts or behavioural issues
- Maintaining records, including data collection
- Operating or assisting in the operation of technology, including computers, smartboards, assistive technology, and other electronic equipment
- Working as part of a multidisciplinary team to provide meaningful instruction and carry out therapeutic programs under the direction of consultants such as speech-language pathologists, psychologists, and others
- Administering standardized tests (but not interpreting the results)
- Assisting the school in meeting the supervisory, cultural, social, and emotional learning goals of all students

The EA is not responsible for instruction or assessment of students, or communication with families, consultants, or specialists. However, the EA may participate in these activities at the direction of the teacher.

## What Do You Think?

Fatima, Jay, Chris, and Jeannie are EAs working at different schools. Below are descriptions of their typical days at work.

What roles do these EAs play in their classrooms and in their schools more broadly?

1. Fatima works in a junior high school, supporting students in grades 7, 8, and 9. This term she is assigned to work with the math department, supporting students during instructional time. She sometimes works one-on-one with each of a particular group of four students who have ongoing struggles in mathematics. At other times, she is available to an entire class, answering students' questions as they learn a new concept. One hour each morning, Fatima, who speaks Arabic, helps three refugee students from Syria who have recently arrived at the school. She answers their questions and helps them to understand their class schedules, organize their books, dress appropriately for Canadian winters, and learn basic English vocabulary. She is also able to connect with their families by being a familiar, welcoming face at the school.

2. This year, Jay works in a class of 28 grade 4 students. His particular assignment is to provide support for two children, Amy and Jake, who are on the autism spectrum. While academic support for his students is very important, Jay also prioritizes opportunities for social development. In conjunction with the classroom teacher he orchestrates learning activities that allow Amy and Jake chances to interact with other students. Jay also goes outside for recess with the students, as this is an important opportunity to facilitate meaningful social interactions. Occasionally, Amy has physical outbursts. It is Jay's role to support Amy through these outbursts and teach her strategies to calm herself.

3. Chris works one-on-one with Drake, a boy in grade 10 who has a cognitive delay. To accommodate Drake's learning needs, Chris modifies the curriculum. In his grade 10 geometry class, Drake manipulates shapes from a wooden geometric puzzle. In consultation with the classroom teacher, Chris orchestrates opportunities for Drake to interact with other students in the class. Chris also assists Drake with personal care tasks such as toileting and putting on his shoes and jacket.

4. Jeannie is employed in an elementary school. Her primary role is to support emergent readers in division 1. Under the supervision of a teacher, Jeannie uses various strategies to support the learning of decoding and comprehension skills. Sometimes she takes individual or small groups of students to the library to practice reading skills. Other times, she supervises whole classes as they work on an assignment, freeing the teacher to work at the back of the room with a small group of students. Jeannie also supervises students in the lunchroom, during lunch break and recesses, and as they board the bus at dismissal.

## To Whom Are EAs Accountable?

The individuals to whom an EA is professionally accountable will depend on the specifics of their position and the children they work with.

Teachers have primary responsibility for the educational program and curriculum of a class. They assign and supervise the work of the EA. Where EAs work with more than one teacher, they are accountable to each of them. If an EA is responsible for attending to a student's medical needs as well as assisting the teacher in the classroom, the EA would report to both the teacher and a healthcare professional or therapist who works with the child.

## The Effective EA

An effective EA is able to connect with others and be flexible. The EA must be able to build collaborative working relationships with students, teachers, families, and other members of the team. This implies warmth and empathy. The effective EA is able to respond quickly to situations and people, has excellent problem-solving skills, and can maintain a sense of humour under chaotic conditions.

The effective EA is sensitive to cultures and abilities, pays attention to individual learning needs and behaviours, and is patient and understanding while managing children whose behaviours are challenging. The EA needs to be enthusiastic about the job and have plenty of energy and strength to perform required physical tasks.

The effective EA will take initiative but have a good sense for boundaries. They will recognize that some teachers welcome suggestions, while others do not. The EA may be placed in several classrooms in the course of a day, and each classroom may have different rules. The EA needs to be perceptive in order to slide seamlessly into these various situations.

EAs may possess many valuable skills and it's important that schools take advantage of these. Individual EAs may bring specific skills, such as fluency in more than one language, including sign language or braille, nonviolent crisis intervention training, first aid training, or previous experience as a healthcare worker. It's to the advantage of EAs to take every possible opportunity to upgrade their existing skills and develop new ones. As one veteran EA advised, "Learn everything you can."

The effective EA's work is grounded in a firm set of beliefs and values. Foremost among these are the beliefs that everyone is unique and valuable and contributes to the world in their own way, that everyone has a story to tell, and that all children have a right to have the support they need to develop to their full potential. The effective EA is committed to helping provide that support.

# Ethical Conduct

As an Educational Assistant, you have an obligation to uphold ethical standards of conduct. Check to see if there is a code of conduct in your jurisdiction that defines specific standards for EAs. Generally speaking, ethical conduct has to do with your duties to students, other EAs, your supervising teacher(s), families, educational authorities, members of the public, and (if applicable) members of your union. The following points, adapted from the CUPE (n.d.) Code of Ethics for Educational Assistants and Youth Service Workers, lay out some common aspects of ethical conduct to keep in mind.

## Duties to Students

As an EA, you should:
- Promote an atmosphere of respect for children and adults
- Promote an atmosphere that fosters independence for students
- Treat students in a respectful, responsible, and fair manner with due consideration of the students' physical, psychological, social, and emotional development
- Refuse to divulge, beyond your legal obligations, confidential information about a student
- Concern yourself with the welfare of your students while they are under your care
- Be an advocate for the rights of your student(s) in school and, where possible, in public
- Regard the dignity, liberty and integrity of each student under your supervision and endeavour to convey to your students an understanding of their own worth

## Duties to Members of Your Profession

As an EA, you should:

- Promote and advance the cause of education and integration of students with exceptionalities
- Build awareness as to the important contributions of EAs
- Participate cooperatively whenever acting as a member of your school-based team
- Not criticize the professional competence or professional reputation of a colleague except to proper authorities, and then only in confidence and according to proper procedures for reporting
- Strive to be supportive of other EAs
- Demonstrate an appropriate and independent use of time in the workplace

## Duties to Educational Authorities

As an EA, you should:

- Cooperate with teachers and administrators to improve integration and education of students
- Report through proper channels and according to proper procedures all matters harmful to the welfare of students

## Duties to the Public

As an EA, you should:

- Recognize your responsibility to promote respect for human rights
- Show respect for law, authority, and codes of conduct acceptable within the profession, school, and society as a whole

# Professional Attitudes and Behaviours

Your ethical obligation includes a responsibility to represent your profession in a responsible manner. Acting like a professional means:

- Showing others that you are reliable
  - › Always being on time
  - › Following through on promises
  - › Completing work by or before the deadline

- Being respectful, kind, and courteous; treating people like they matter
- Displaying competence by doing your job well
- Being honest, positive, and helpful

- Respecting confidentiality
  › Not sharing information about students, families, teachers, or the school with anyone not authorized to have that information

## Confidentiality

Maintaining confidentiality is critical. You are in a position to know a great deal about many children and families. You have a responsibility to keep that information safe and private, as do the teachers and consultants who are working directly with those children. You can imagine how you would feel if someone revealed private information about your child or family without your consent. For someone to share this information would be a violation of your trust, and would certainly damage your relationship with them.

There are legal implications about when and how sensitive information can be shared. Privacy legislation varies from province to province. Check your school's policies and, if you are in doubt, consult your principal.

# Professionalism Case Studies

It is one thing to know your professional obligations and expectations, and another to put them into practice. Consider the case studies that follow and examples of the ways in which an EA might respond professionally or unprofessionally.

**Practicing Professionalism: Scenario 1**

**Scenario 1.** The class was very excited about a mosaic they had made. It turned out beautifully and the students were thrilled. You were also pleased that the mural turned out so well.

| UNPROFESSIONAL RESPONSE | PROFESSIONAL RESPONSE |
|---|---|
| • Take a photo of the mural on your camera and paste it on social media so your friends can see it. | • Ask the classroom teacher if he would like you to take a photo of the mural on the class's tablet and post it on the class's website for families to see. |

**Practicing Professionalism: Scenario 2**

**Scenario 2.** It was a rough morning in your classroom. Your cooperating teacher confided in you that he was walking the floor with his newborn all night. He was low on energy and was having trouble keeping up with the class.

| UNPROFESSIONAL RESPONSES | PROFESSIONAL RESPONSES |
|---|---|
| • Tell the other staff members during recess about your difficult morning.<br>• Mention the teacher's struggles to the families when they come to pick up their children. | • Do your best to anticipate the needs of the teacher, providing support as is appropriate.<br>• Pay extra close attention to the students in the class, anticipating their needs and supporting their learning. |

# Knowing Emergency Policies and Procedures

One of the first things you must do as a new EA is familiarize yourself with the school's policies and procedures. These may include protocols for lockdowns, pandemics, earthquakes, fires, and other emergencies. In the event of an emergency, your first responsibility is to ensure the safety of the children. From there, you must follow school protocols and adhere to communication procedures.

An emergency situation could occur at any time. It is therefore important to thoroughly familiarize yourself with your school's policies and procedures right from the start of your employment.

Consider, for example, the emergency procedures you may need to follow if there is an intruder in your school. The following lockdown procedure is typical:

## Practicing Professionalism: Scenario 3

**Scenario 3.** One of the students became very frustrated during a group activity you were supervising. She threw her markers onto the floor. Very upset, she shouted, "You never listen to me! I hate this group. I want to be in a different group."

| UNPROFESSIONAL RESPONSES | PROFESSIONAL RESPONSES |
|---|---|
| • Insist the student write an apology letter to her group then read it to them.<br>• Phone the student's family and tell them about the incident.<br>• Tell your friends about the incident. | • Use your behaviour intervention skills to support the children as they resolve their conflict.<br>• Tell the teacher about the conflict at the earliest opportunity.<br>• Document the incident. |

- Everyone goes immediately to the room they are closest to.
- If a child is in the washroom, they must lock themselves in a stall or go to the nearest open classroom.
- The teacher or EA closes the curtains and locks the door.
- The children sit against the wall furthest from the window and are quiet.
- The teacher or EA takes attendance; as an EA, you need to know which children should be in the room at that time.

In an emergency situation such as this, you must be able to respond immediately. There is no time to check on procedures.

# Possible Challenges

It will certainly be challenging at times for EAs to respond to the many demands and personalities they will encounter in their work. Since EAs are often assigned to work with students who have challenging behaviours, you are likely to encounter such behaviours often. A demanding workload and conflicting requests from teachers and supervisors can cause stress. The same is true of the lack of a fully defined job description: an EA plays many roles, and could always be asked to play one more. Because of all of these factors, the abilities to recognize signs of physical or mental stress, problem solve, and ask for help are critical.

Given all of the relationships that the EA navigates every day, it's easy to see why the EA position is sometimes described as "liminal." The *Canadian Oxford Dictionary* defines *liminal* as "occupying a position at, or on both sides of, a boundary or threshold" (Barber, 2004). On one hand, the EA is responsible to the teacher and school, and indirectly to the families. On the other hand, the EA has tremendous power to shape children's school experiences. At school, the EA is often the person who knows a child best and is able to respond sensitively and patiently to that child's needs.

Even though the EA may be assigned to work with one child, unless that child is in need of constant care, the EA moves throughout the classroom and sometimes to different rooms in the school. This means the EA will have the opportunity to build relationships with many children as they work to support the inclusion of all students.

You will have noticed that the section on professional ethics mentions your responsibility to advocate for the rights of students in the school and in public. Advocacy is an important aspect of the work of an EA, and will be discussed more fully in Chapter 4.

## Takeaways

- *Educational assistant* is one of several possible titles for a position that provides support to teachers in school or other settings.
- EAs may have a variety of different responsibilities depending on the needs of the school and their particular skills.
- EAs are expected to behave ethically and professionally, according to the standards, policies, and procedures of the jurisdiction and school in which they work.
- It is important that EAs become familiar with policies and procedures in their schools, including emergency protocols.

## Reflection and Discussion

Francine, the EA from the beginning of this chapter, was asked the following questions at her interview. If you were the person being interviewed, how would you answer each of these?

- Why are you interested in working as an EA?
- What qualities, skills, and experiences would you bring to an EA position?
- What would you do if a parent complained to you about something the teacher did?
- What would you do if your best friend asked you for information about the family of a child with whom you are working?
- What aspects of an EA position might be the most challenging for you?
- What aspects of an EA position do you think you would be strongest in?

# The Educational Assistant as Advocate

*Act as if what you do makes a difference. It does.*

—*WILLIAM JAMES*

### Learning Outcomes

After reading this chapter, you will be able to answer these questions:

- What does it mean to be an advocate?
- Why is advocacy an important role for EAs to take on?
- How can you become a successful advocate?
- What should you do if you suspect that a child is being abused or neglected?

## Introduction

In your work as an EA, there will be times when you need to be an advocate for children, for yourself, for your profession, or for a larger cause. Knowing how to advocate effectively is an important skill for you as an EA.

This chapter looks at the different advocacy roles you will play as an EA, and strategies fill those roles effectively.

## When Might You Advocate?

As an EA, you will act as an advocate for students and help them learn to advocate for themselves. This advocacy role could include supporting the teacher in finding appropriate resources to assist students and their families or joining movements that ask for such resources at a broader societal level. It might also involve responding to disclosures or suspicions of abuse or neglect.

It's also important to know how to advocate for yourself and for your profession. Being an EA can be a stressful job, and it's important that you and your colleagues have the supports you need to be successful in your work.

Consider the four situations below:

1. You've seen how Cassidy struggles with math. "I'm so stupid," she says, "I'm trying and trying but I can't do this." You believe that she should be tested for an exceptionality, but the teacher hasn't put her name forward for testing.

2. You are assigned to work with Jake, a 12-year-old boy who has behaviour disorders. He can be quite violent at times, throwing desks, pushing people, and otherwise endangering other students. When Jake is having a dangerous outburst, the teacher takes the other children to the library and you are left alone with Jake. He is a very strong, big student, and you don't feel safe being left alone with him at these times.

3. The new recess schedule leaves most of the EAs at your school with a 15-minute lunch break.

4. You join an organization that is lobbying for better access to public buildings for people with exceptionalities.

Any one of these situations might call for you to act as an advocate—that is, to speak up for a particular cause. You might be advocating with the teacher to have Cassidy tested for an exceptionality, or to have some kind of backup when Jake has a dangerous episode. You and other EAs might join together as a group to suggest alternatives to the 15-minute lunch break. The organization lobbying for better access is depending on gathering a large group of people to their cause, knowing there is strength in numbers.

## Becoming an Advocate for Students

As an EA, your first concern is always the student. Sometimes, as in scenario 1 above, you may feel that a student's educational, social-emotional, medical, or other needs are not being met appropriately. How can you advocate for Cassidy in a way that is both professional and effective?

## Be a Credible Team Member

First of all, think of how you are positioning yourself as part of the school. If your colleagues see you as a committed, effective, and enthusiastic member of the school team, you will have greater credibility when you raise an issue.

Here are some things you can do to establish that reputation:

- Form positive relationships with everyone on staff and show interest in things that are happening at the school. Smile, be kind, volunteer, and don't make complaints in an unprofessional manner. People are more likely to listen when they see you as a contributing member of the school community.
- Deal with conflict effectively so that children don't get caught in the middle. Try to see all sides of an issue.
- Be positive and upbeat about the students.
- Maintain professional behaviour at all times; for example, never communicate negative feelings about the school or a colleague to students or families.
- Convey the attitude that inclusive education is good for all students, not just those with exceptionalities.
- Understand the chain of responsibility. In scenario 1 above, you are accountable to the teacher, so the teacher is the person to whom you should bring your concerns about Cassidy. The teacher, in turn, is responsible to the principal, and the principal to the superintendent.

## Know Your Resources

An important part of preparing yourself to advocate for children is knowing what resources are available in the community to assist students from different backgrounds and students with exceptionalities, as well as their families. Research organizations, not-for-profits, and advocacy groups in your area that focus on particular populations and exceptionalities can be a great resource. Depending on the challenges you are handling in your work, you may look for organizations or groups that focus on and offer services around:

- Indigenous Peoples' issues
- Refugees and other newcomers to Canada
- Drug addictions
- Teen pregnancies
- Homelessness
- Eating disorders
- Autism
- Down syndrome

- Fetal alcohol spectrum disorder (FASD)
- Cerebral palsy
- Deafness and hearing loss
- Blindness and visual impairment
- Diabetes
- Cancer
- Crohn's disease
- Epilepsy

Knowing about these organizations and services makes you a valuable resource to the school and to families, adding to your ability and credibility as an advocate.

# Advocating for Children Who Are Being Neglected or Abused

Children who are being neglected or abused are very much in need of your assistance, but you must be an informed advocate who knows the appropriate responses and procedures. Otherwise, you run the risk of doing more harm than good. Protocols for detecting and reporting child abuse and neglect will vary from province to province. Different school boards may also have their own protocols. It is essential that you are familiar with the protocols relevant to your place of work.

## What Are Neglect and Abuse?[3]

The Government of Alberta (n.d.) provides useful definitions of neglect and emotional, physical, and sexual abuse, along with the warning signs to watch for.

### Neglect

A child or youth is considered to be neglected when a parent or guardian does not provide them with basic, age-appropriate care such as food, clothing, shelter, love and affection, and protection from harm. Neglected children and youth may:

- Often be hungry and steal or hoard food
- Be underweight or dehydrated
- Have poor hygiene
- Wear clothes that are torn, dirty, do not fit, or are not right for the season

---

[3] Information in this section is adapted from the Government of Alberta (n.d.).

- Try to take on age-inappropriate responsibilities (such as caring for siblings and doing household tasks when very young, or looking after a parent)
- Say that their parents are rarely home or that they don't want to go home
- Have medical or dental problems that will not go away, such as infected sores, decayed teeth, or vision difficulties that are not being addressed

## Emotional abuse

Emotional abuse of a child can happen along with neglect or the other types of abuse. An emotional abuser may:
- Humiliate the child by blaming or belittling them
- Refuse to comfort the child when the child is upset or frightened
- Criticize the child by calling them stupid, bad, useless, or a troublemaker
- Set unrealistic expectations, threaten or accuse the child
- Expose the child to violence or chronic drug or alcohol use in the home
- Give cruel or unusual treatment or punishment

An emotionally abused child or youth may:
- Constantly apologize or try too hard to please others
- Show anxiety, fears, or depression
- Have trouble concentrating, learning, or sleeping
- Have episodes of aggressive, angry, and demanding behaviour
- Cry for no apparent reason
- Have problems with bed-wetting or fecal incontinence

## Physical abuse

A child is considered to be physically abused when a parent or guardian causes an injury or trauma to any part of the child's body. The abuse might leave bruises and marks that can be seen, but can also include internal injuries that are hard to spot. Physical abuse can happen only once or many times. It may include:
- Hitting, choking, and kicking
- Biting, scratching, and pulling hair
- Throwing or hitting their child with things
- Breaking bones

A physically abused child or youth may have visible injuries or illness that are unexplained or poorly explained, including:

- Bruises, cuts, scrapes, welts, fractures, sprains, dislocations, or head injuries
- Injuries that could not have happened by accident, like a bruised earlobe or a cut behind the knee
- Visible handprints, fingerprints, or other marks
- Burns on various parts of their body
- Unusual behaviour or appearance
- X-ray results that indicate prior injuries

In addition, the child or youth may:

- Be defensive about their injuries
- Wear clothing that covers their body even when the weather is warm
- Not be able to tolerate physical contact or touch
- Fear their parents/guardians or other adults
- Run away
- Be reluctant to undress around others
- Say their parent or guardian has injured them

### Sexual abuse

Sexual abuse happens when a parent or guardian exposes their child to or does not protect their child or youth from inappropriate sexual contact, activity, or behaviour. This may include:

- Activities that do not involve sexual touch, such as:
  › Having inappropriately sexual phone calls or conversations
  › Making the child watch someone expose themselves
  › Showing the child pornographic material

- Sexual touching activities such as:
  › Fondling
  › Making the child touch an adult's or other child's genital area
  › Sexual intercourse with the child or youth

- Sexual exploitation activities such as:
  › Engaging in prostitution of a child
  › Offering a child or youth for prostitution
  › Using a child in pornography
  › Luring a child via the Internet for sexual purposes

A sexually abused child or youth may:

- Show more knowledge about sex than others their age
- Behave in an improper or aggressively sexual way with peers, teachers, EAs, or other adults
- Use sexual language or make drawings with sexual images
- Start wetting or soiling their pants, wetting the bed, or thumb-sucking
- Be afraid to go to sleep, have nightmares, or sleep long hours
- Become withdrawn, anxious, fearful, or depressed
- Have physical trauma or irritations in the anal and genital areas

## Handling Disclosures and Suspicions of Neglect or Abuse

If a child discloses or hints at being neglected or abused by anyone, there are some important dos and don'ts to follow.

**TABLE 4.1. Dos and Don'ts of Handling Disclosures of Abuse or Neglect**

| DOS | DON'TS |
|---|---|
| • Do listen calmly.<br>• Do tell the child that they have done the right thing in telling you, and that they have done nothing wrong. Let the child know that you have to tell their teacher what they have told you.<br>• Do document both what the child has said and what you have observed. Share this with your supervising teacher immediately. | • Don't probe for details or encourage the child to share details.<br>• Don't ask the child to repeat their story to you or to the supervising teacher or other trusted adults. This could be hard on the child and make the process more difficult down the line.<br>• Don't discuss your concerns with the child's parents as this can interfere with an investigation. |
| For the protection of the child and the possible apprehension and prosecution of the offender, it is very important that the incident be reported to the appropriate authorities, and that the child be carefully questioned by a highly skilled investigator who knows how to gather and evaluate the evidence. | |

Even if a child has not disclosed an incident of neglect or abuse to you, but you have observed signs of abuse or neglect, it's important to carefully document what you have observed and share it with your supervising teacher.

# Helping Students Learn to Advocate for Themselves

An important skill that students will need to have by the time they transition from school is the ability to advocate for themselves. They need to know how to identify their own needs, speak up for themselves, problem-solve, ask for help when they need it, and listen to others. Preparing children to be self-advocates can begin early and have sizable benefits. The child who is able to self-advocate develops independence, self-confidence, and self-efficacy. The actions you take to help a student with exceptionalities learn self-advocacy can be beneficial to all children. These include:

- Helping students develop a realistic picture of their personal interests, preferences, strengths, and limitations
- Helping students understand the conditions and support they need in order to learn best
- Involving students in setting their own educational goals
- Encouraging students to speak up
- Teaching problem-solving skills and giving students time to solve problems on their own
- Reminding students that people learn in different ways

By helping students develop these skills and this knowledge, you are helping them build a strong and thoughtful voice, and a perspective from which they can understand both their challenges and their possibilities.

# Advocating for Yourself

EAs work with some of the most vulnerable students and in situations that are occasionally dangerous. This makes it especially important that you be able to advocate for yourself.

Self-advocacy can be easier when you already have a reputation for being a positive and competent presence in your school. In addition, you should aim to:

- Build and maintain your credibility as a professional who is part of the staff team
- Get involved with professional development activities and organizations
- Know your rights
- Familiarize yourself with the school's policy on violence in the workplace and whether it applies to students with exceptionalities
- Cultivate your self-awareness and maintain your life balance

- Always remember the importance of the work you are doing
- Learn as much as you can about the system within which you work

Being prepared in these ways will ensure that you have the credibility, confidence, and information to effectively advocate for yourself when it's important to do so.

## The Art of Persuasion

You've decided to speak up about your concerns and advocate for a student, for yourself, or for a larger cause. How can you increase your chances of getting results? Here are some tips to help you navigate the conversation:

- *Be prepared.* Support your argument with documentation and/or research. Think of objections that might be raised and be prepared to respond to them.
- *Be calm and respectful.* Convey your willingness to engage with the other person to come to a solution.
- *Have a solution (or more than one solution) in mind.* Show how your idea benefits what is at issue (e.g., the child, the school, the teacher).
- *Be open to listening to the other's views.* Acknowledge points of view that are raised that you hadn't thought about.
- *Be willing to compromise.* Be open to finding a solution that accommodates the needs of others, too.
- *Don't force an immediate decision.* Agree to return to the discussion later.

Pay attention to when and where you have this kind of conversation. If this is a one-to-one conversation, for example, it's usually best to pick a place where the other person can feel comfortable, and to speak at a time when the other person isn't feeling hurried or distracted.

Advocacy stems from your awareness of a cause and your commitment to creating change. It requires that you have an accurate picture of the situation, have identified possible actions to remedy it, and know how best to be heard. The ability to understand and think through these situations takes practice.

Chapter 5 provides you with a process for reflective practice to help you think through puzzling situations. Reflective practice is an important tool for learning and professional growth.

## Takeaways

- EAs need to develop advocacy skills in order to meet the needs of students, look after themselves, and contribute to the wellbeing of society.
- You may advocate for yourself (self-advocacy), for an individual, or for a group.
- Learning to self-advocate is an important skill for all children, but particularly students with exceptionalities. It is also an important skill for you, as an EA.
- Building credibility as a staff member will increase your effectiveness as an advocate.

 ## Reflection and Discussion

- Can you think of a time when you have advocated for others? A time when you have advocated for yourself?
- This chapter includes some examples of situations in a school setting that might require either individual or group advocacy. Can you think of other examples that might prompt advocacy in a school setting?
- What personal skills and attributes do you possess that help you be an effective advocate? Which might you want to develop?

## 5

# Introduction to Reflective Practice

*Follow effective action with quiet reflection. From the quiet reflection will come even more effective action.*

—PETER DRUCKER

### Learning Outcomes

After reading this chapter, you will be able to answer these questions:

- What do we mean by reflective practice?
- Why is reflective practice important to professional development?
- How can you become more reflective in your professional and personal life?
- Why is it important to become aware of your unconscious biases?

## Introduction

Reflective practice is a valuable tool for ongoing professional learning. This chapter includes a structured process for working through puzzling situations. You won't need to follow this precise process in every situation in order to be a reflective practitioner, but it will help you to be aware of the steps involved in working through a problem. Being aware of your own biases ensures that you are seeing situations and possible solutions as objectively you can. This chapter concludes with an exercise to help you become aware of biases that might stand in the way of your learning and relationships.

# What Is Reflective Practice?

Reflective process can benefit all aspects of your work as an EA. It can help you learn the strategies that work and don't work with particular children. It can also help you identify your own biggest challenges and learn how to face them. Through reflective practice, you can also form closer relationships with students, families, and colleagues.

> "I'm so frustrated," Maya sighs. "I just can't get the grade 8 group to listen to me. They aren't allowed to have their phones but all they want to do is talk about the computer game they're playing outside of school. How can reading and writing compete with that?"

Reflective practice is a tool for resolving puzzling situations like the one Maya describes. The practice of reflection creates new understandings to take into future situations. In that way, it allows for ongoing professional growth.

Reflective practice involves paying deliberate and critical attention to everyday events and actions in a way that can lead to learning. It involves an attitude, a habit, and a skill:

- *Attitude*: wanting to continually improve
- *Habit*: taking the time to think deeply about day-to-day experiences
- *Skill*: being able to reflect in a way that allows for continuous learning from our professional experiences

Maya uses her reflective practice to get curious about the challenges she is experiencing with her grade 8 students. She asks herself some questions to better understand the situation and the ways in which she can improve the situation through the role she plays in it. Thinking through these questions will allow Maya to develop a course of action.

### Should I ask the teacher what to do?

The teacher will be a great resource, but Maya wants to understand the problem and have a plan of action to suggest to the teacher before she goes to her.

### Do the students not feel connected to me?

Maya has only been working with these particular students for two weeks and feels like she doesn't know them very well. They may feel the same way about her. Perhaps more time is needed to develop a connection.

### Is this reading material that I have for this group too advanced? Too boring?

In this group, the students are reading at a grade 3–4 level. The materials Maya has chosen to use with them are at that reading level. However, she wonders if the content of these materials interesting for this group of older students.

### Are there too many distracting things going on around us while we work?

Maya works with this group in a quiet corner of the library and the students seem more interested in their own discussions than in what is going on around them.

### What do I know about the computer game they're playing?

Maya knows a bit about computer games but not the one the students are playing. She decides to ask someone who might know more: her teenage nephew!

---

After thinking through these questions and researching the computer game with her nephew, Maya develops a plan of action. She decides that she will tap into the students' interest in the currently popular computer game. She will ask them to explain it to her, which will help build her relationship with them. From there, she will propose that, as a group, they compose a story about the adventures of the main character in their game. In doing this, she will draw upon the strengths of the individual students. She will, for example, ask the artistic student who struggles the most with reading to illustrate the book. There is also one quiet but highly imaginative student whom she suspects will contribute to an excellent story line. Maya will show the students how to bind the book and they'll put it in the school library.

Think about the steps Maya took in her reflective practice in the example above. The most important thing that Maya did was take time to think through the problem she was facing. When Maya took the time to think, she was able to pay attention to her feelings and to be open to considering many possible reasons for her students' inattention. In the end, this led her to a creative solution that addressed several of her questions. In exploring the problem, Maya generated a number of possibilities, then consulted her teenage nephew who knows all about computer games. Later, when she shared her ideas with her mentor teacher, the teacher suggested expanding her idea to include reading to the younger children.

As a result of her reflective process, Maya has constructed an engaging experience that will develop the children's literacy skills, highlight their individual strengths, and build their confidence in their abilities. She keeps her teacher informed of the students' progress and the teacher arranges for these students to read their book to children in the lower grades as part of the school reading program.

## The Process of Reflection

Developing the attitude, habit, and skill of reflective practice involves developing qualities such as the following:

- *Self-awareness*: the ability to pay attention to your thoughts and feelings
- *Creativity*: the ability to brainstorm many alternative explanations
- *Honesty*: the ability to recognize the assumptions and biases that might be affecting your analysis and evaluation of the situation
- *Openness*: willingness to explore the possibility of other perspectives; for example, cultural beliefs and practices that are different from your own
- *Motivation*: the willingness to commit time and energy to ongoing self-reflection

Developing these qualities doesn't happen overnight. Even taking the time to reflect and think deeply can be challenging in itself. EAs are in demand for many different tasks at their school and are accountable to a number of people. Often, EAs are so busy that "just thinking" seems like a waste of time. As we saw in Maya's example above, however, learning how to take this time and use it well can be invaluable to an EA's success.

When you are new to reflective practice, it can be useful, at first, to have a step-by-step process to follow to help you practice the movements of reflective practice until they become second nature. We call this process *the reflective practice cycle*.

### The Reflective Practice Cycle

The reflective practice cycle involves fives steps:

1. *Describe* the event to yourself and any others that you enlist for assistance in as objective and accurate a manner as possible.

2. *Reflect* on your reaction to the event. Be in touch with the thoughts and feelings you have during and after the event. Sometimes, it's your feeling of unease that alerts you to the fact that there actually is a problem. Your thoughts and feelings are also a way to learn about

yourself. For example, they can help you uncover unconscious biases you have towards some aspect of the event that are affecting the way you respond.

3. *Explore* the event. Ask questions to better understand the broader context of the event. Come up with many different possibilities to explain why the event has happened. You could talk with more experienced colleagues or search through resources.

4. *Evaluate* the possibilities you've generated and decide which is or are the more likely explanations for the event.

5. *Act* on a solution that responds to your new understanding of the event. Reflect on the efficacy of your solution, and take your learning with you, to help you if the event ever happens again: make it a part of your practice.

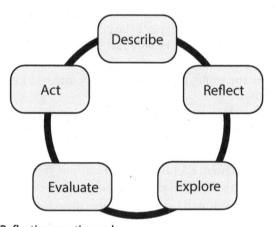

FIGURE 5.1. Reflective practice cycle

Let's look at another example to better understand the steps in the reflective practice cycle.

> Amanda, an EA, has just started working with Tyler, a nonverbal child. Today, when it was time to go to the gym, Tyler became very upset and was physically aggressive towards Amanda. Amanda is, at first, unsure how to respond.

In the following section, Amanda uses the reflective practice cycle to better understand this puzzling situation, and to come up with a solution.

### Describe

Amanda accurately describes the situation to herself:

> When I asked Tyler to go to the gym, he threw a book at me and tried to bite me.

### Reflect

She reflects on the thoughts, feelings, and behaviours that were involved in her reaction to this situation:

> At the time, I was puzzled and a bit frightened. I found myself thinking, "You little brat! What have I ever done to you!" I backed away from him to avoid getting bit.

### Explore

Amanda takes the time to think about why Tyler may have reacted in the way that he did. She considers the situation from different angles, and asks for input from colleagues who are familiar with Tyler's behaviours and needs:

> - Does Tyler usually react violently when asked to go to the gym? Ask his teacher and his former EA.
>
> - Did I approach him in the wrong way? Ask his teacher and his former EA.
>
> - Is something else bothering Tyler today? Check with his teacher about the rest of Tyler's day.
>
> - Has something happened in the gym before to upset him? Check with his former EA.
>
> - Is Tyler not feeling well today?

### Evaluate

Amanda gathers the information she has learned, and comes to a deeper understanding of the situation:

> I learned that Tyler had had a bad morning. His family was out of his usual breakfast cereal and this was very upsetting for him. Then he had to rush to get to his bus on time. Changes to his routine are very hard for Tyler.

*Act*

Amanda comes up with a solution that she thinks will respond to the larger situation surrounding Tyler's behaviour, and monitors the success of this solution:

> To show him I understand, I will talk with Tyler about his disappointment about breakfast. Perhaps he will draw me a picture of his feelings.
>
> I will observe and reflect on this action to see if I'm on the right track in responding to Tyler's moods.

As you become more skilled at using reflective practice, you probably won't need to follow the steps of this cycle as closely as Amanda does. However, any time you find yourself in a particularly difficult situation, or feel especially stuck, remembering these five steps can help guide you to a solution.

## Managing Bias

Reflective practice requires an ability to be objective about people and events. Biases can hinder our ability to be objective. We all have biases and we need to work to become aware of them to prevent them from entering into our interactions and decision-making.

Bias is the tendency to favour one thing over another. Biases can be positive; for example, we may have a bias toward certain kinds of healthy food, or toward offering pregnant women our seat on the bus.

More often, though, we think about bias in connection with stereotypes. That is, our biases can lead us to make judgements without having actual knowledge of a person or situation. For example, we might assume that all people who are of Asian descent are good at math.

We all have biases. Psychologists refer to them as "cognitive shortcuts" or ways to quickly make sense of the world. Usually these biases are shaped by the experiences, values, and beliefs we hold, as well as by the influence of our friends, family, and education. Sometimes we are aware of our biases and sometimes they are unconscious.

If we are aware of our biases, we can bring that awareness to our interactions and our decision-making processes. If we know that we are biased against certain beliefs or lifestyles, acknowledging that bias allows us to be open to experiences that might challenge our ideas about that particular group.

Unconscious bias, however, limits our ability to learn about other ways of being, form relationships with those different from ourselves, and make decisions based on many possibilities. It's important that we work to become conscious of our biases relating to factors such as appearance, age, family structure, socioeconomic status, religion, language, abilities, ethnicity, gender, or sexual orientation.

## What Do You Think?

What unconscious biases do you hold? These are a few questions to help you think and talk about your biases.

### Appearance

- Do you prefer certain physical characteristics such as hair colour, skin tone, height, body shape?
- Are there mannerisms that bother you?

### Age

- Do you feel some individuals have certain beliefs, responsibilities, or capabilities based on their age?

### Family structure

- What is your picture of the "ideal" family?
- Do you believe that lone parent families have more challenges than two parent families?
- What are your views on same-sex families?

### Socioeconomic status

- Do you believe that children who live in poverty can have a happy childhood?
- Do you believe that children from higher-income families tend to need more attention from their parents?

### Religion

- Do you believe that some religions or forms of spirituality are better than others?
- How do you feel about persons who profess to have no religion?
- Do you associate certain actions or values with particular religions?

### Language

- Do you believe that individuals who don't speak English well are less intelligent?
- How do you feel about sexist or racist language?

### Abilities

- How comfortable do you feel around people who have physical or intellectual exceptionalities?
- Are there particular ways you feel you should talk or act with these individuals?

### Ethnicity, race, and Indigenous ancestry

- What assumptions do you make about people of a particular race or ethnicity?
- What assumptions do you make about people of Indigenous ancestry?
- Do you have specific ideas about the foods people of different ancestry eat? the clothes they wear? their customs, beliefs, or lifestyles?

### Gender identity and sexual orientation

- What are your beliefs about the roles of males and females?
- What assumptions do you make about the way a person's gender identity relates to their sexual orientation?
- How do you feel about individuals who identify as lesbian, gay, bisexual, transgender, two-spirited, queer, or sexually fluid?

---

Remember: Just because you have unconscious biases doesn't necessarily mean you have to change them. It is, however, important to be aware of these biases so that it is less likely that they will unconsciously interfere with your relationships and decisions.

In other words, knowing your biases helps you to be more objective in your descriptions and in generating possibilities—essential aspects of reflective practice. The deep thought involved in reflective practice can, in turn, help you be more aware of biases.

We will be mentioning the role of bias again in Chapter 6, when we consider the web of relationships in which you, as an EA, will be involved.

**Takeaways**

- The habit of ongoing reflection allows you to continue your learning throughout your career as an EA. It is an ongoing form of professional development.
- Using a structured process for reflection enables you to think systematically about puzzling situations.
- There are particular qualities that are important for reflective practice, including self-awareness, creativity, honesty, openness, and motivation
- Reflective practice can help us become aware of our unconscious biases because it encourages us to be open to many different possibilities. At the same time, being aware of our biases helps us to be objective in working with people and situations.

 **Reflection and Discussion**

- How would you explain the value of reflective practice?
- What are the characteristics of a reflective EA?
- How could reflection support your work as an EA?
- How could the practice of reflection help you in your everyday life?
- Think about a puzzling situation or event that you've experienced and try working through it using the reflective practice cycle.

# 6

# A Practice of Relationships

*Too often we underestimate the power of a touch,
a smile, a kind word, a listening ear, an honest
compliment, or the smallest act of caring, all of
which have the potential to turn a life around.*

—*LEO F. BUSCAGLIA*

## Learning Outcomes

After reading this chapter, you will be able to answer these questions:

- Why do we call the work that an EA does a *practice of relationships*?
- Why is it particularly important to have strong, trusting relationships with children?
- What are some ways that EAs can support children in building connections with one another?
- What are some things that EAs can do to facilitate their working relationships with teachers?
- Why is it important to be aware of boundaries in your relationships with families?

## Introduction

In Chapter 3, we discussed some of the possible duties an EA might perform at their place of work. Did you notice all of the different people you might interact with in the course of a day? Even if you have been assigned to support a particular child, you will be moving around the classroom or perhaps even to several classrooms. You may be working one-on-one or with groups of children in and out of the classroom. You will be under the direction of a teacher while at the same time providing observations and suggestions to them. Perhaps you will attend a case conference with the teacher and consultants who are involved with your assigned child. The principal might request that you supervise in the playground. You might chat with a family member who is picking up a child with whom you work.

The need to interact effectively with diverse individuals and groups of people is what makes work as an EA a practice of relationships. In this chapter we'll explore the relationships an EA may make and foster with and among students, with teachers, with families, and with other team members.

## Relationships with Children

Your most important relationships as an EA—the ones that can make a lasting difference—are your relationships with the children you work with. All children are vulnerable, but the children that EAs are likely to support are often those that have particular vulnerabilities beyond those of their peers. They might:

- Be struggling to understand what is being taught in class
- Be distracted or angry because of problems at home
- Be coping with bullying in the playground
- Have medical issues that set them apart from their peers
- Be hungry
- See themselves as failures and give up trying

Working one-on-one or in small groups with these children on a regular basis means that the EA is in a position to build trust with them. If the EA is genuinely caring and a good listener, the child may be willing to take the risk of accepting help. The EA becomes an advocate for the child, seeking to support them without betraying their confidence. This support might look like tactfully sharing a snack with a hungry child, or consulting the teacher about an alternative way for a child struggling with coursework to accomplish a learning goal. Perhaps the EA will initiate a playground game that draws other children in and allows an excluded child to excel and belong.

While working with a student, the EA can get to know the student's interests, abilities, personality, and learning style. This knowledge allows the EA to make or suggest adaptations to make the student's learning more effective. Knowing that the EA genuinely cares about their wellbeing and progress gives children feelings of worth and the motivation to succeed.

Some ways that EAs can build positive relationships with children are by:

- Listening
- Observing
- Joining in with their activities
- Sharing information from their own lives
- Planning activities based on the children's interests

## Supporting Peer Relationships

The EA also works to support students' relationships with their peers. This can mean:

- Stepping back so as not to be seen as an extension of the children they are supporting
- Noticing barriers to participation
- Identifying classmates who could be friends
- Planning activities that involve groups of children
- Supporting students in taking leaderships roles in the classroom (e.g., handing out projects)
- Helping children demonstrate their strengths to peers
- Teaching needed social skills
- Providing opportunities for peer support
- Confronting bullying

## Relationships with Teachers

The EA works with and under the guidance of one or more classroom teachers. In the best possible situation, the EA and teacher(s) act as a team, complementing each other's work. They meet regularly to discuss and prepare for lessons, ensuring consistency between their expectations for, and their work with, the children. Their relationship should be collegial, each one trusting the expertise and role of the other. Their relationship should also promote learning from one another: the teacher can act as a mentor to the EA while the EA can share observations about the children and perhaps suggestions about possible adaptations. By watching the teacher, the EA might learn new strategies for dealing with children. The teacher and EA may also support each other by sharing the humour and the heartbreaks that are a part of classroom life.

Unfortunately, there are many barriers that can stand in the way of this ideal situation, perhaps the biggest of which is lack of time. Classrooms are busy places and teachers don't always have or make the time to spend with their EA. This is particularly the case if the EA is working in more than one classroom.

Another barrier that EAs mention is a teacher's inexperience with delegating or reluctance to share classroom responsibilities. This can lead to tension within the teacher/EA relationship, and feelings of being inadequate or unwanted on the part of the EA. Arthur and Annette, two experienced EAs, have this to say:

> I had the feeling that she'd rather not have me there. Maybe she thought I was judging her or something.
>
> —ARTHUR

> I couldn't tell if she thought I was doing a good job or not, and I started feeling very anxious.
>
> —ANNETTE

An EA must learn to recognize their agency in difficult professional situations, and to be flexible to the differing needs and styles of the teacher with whom they work. EAs Parjeet and Carmen offer this advice:

> As support staff you have to follow the teacher's lead. You work differently with each teacher. You have to be flexible and supportive.
>
> —PARJEET

> Some teachers know exactly how they want things done or you have someone who hasn't worked with EAs and doesn't know what they can do. Know the questions to ask to get the information you need to do your job.
>
> —CARMEN

Here are some questions you might ask the teachers with whom you work to help them support you more effectively:
- Is there anything special I should know for today?
- What's your learning goal for this class?
- How would you like me to support you today?
- Would you like me to…?

Sometimes teachers don't know what EAs are capable of doing. It is therefore important to present yourself as a professional and competent presence in the classroom. When appropriate to, walk around the classroom. Offer support and generally demonstrate an attitude of support. Pay attention to students and how they are interacting, feeling, and behaving.

Relationships between EAs and teachers are a two-way street but sometimes EAs will need to take the initiative in order to work effectively. Good communication skills, sensitivity, and self-awareness are essential skills. A sense of humour never hurts, either! Be sensitive to the times when teachers are too busy to talk. Ask, "When is a good time of day for us to discuss…?"

Teachers also need to know that you are seeking advice and anxious to learn. Invite feedback: "If you notice anything that you'd like me to do differently, please let me know."

## Relationships with Families

Communicating with families is the teacher's responsibility, although an EA may share some kinds of information with families at the teacher's discretion. Family members, however, are likely to want to communicate with the EA if the EA is the person who has the most sustained contact with their child at school. Certainly, the EA wants to build a positive relationship with families so they can trust the care that their child is receiving. This relationship, then, is a delicate balancing act in which the EA needs to know how much information to share with the family and when to refer them to the teacher.

Below, an experienced EA shares stories that speak to the boundaries that must be maintained in working with families:

> (The teacher) and I had agreed that M's parents and I would use a communication book to share what was happening for him at home and at school. I would take a few minutes near the end of the day to write in it and send it home with him. His mom asked for my phone number and when I gave it to her, she started calling me in the evenings and on the weekends to talk about his progress and make suggestions. It was more than I could handle, so I told (the teacher) about it. She asked the mom to make contact through the school and explained to me that I shouldn't give my personal phone number to families.
>
> I learned that if you think there might be a concern from the parent, talk to the teacher or the principal quickly and give them a heads up that this happened. It's like documenting. But be aware that you could have made a mistake.

As soon as you begin working with a new teacher, clarify the amount and kind of information you should share with families. This can help to avoid difficult situations later. At the same time, you must be very aware that families of children with exceptionalities may be experiencing a number of challenging feelings: anxiety, protectiveness, guilt, loneliness, anger, even embarrassment. In some cases, the family may be having financial concerns due to unfunded therapy or treatments. Dealing with their child's needs may be putting a strain on their family relationships. Knowing that their child is in a safe environment with someone who really cares about that child can make a tremendous difference to them. Knowing that the teacher and EA are working very closely as a team can be very reassuring.

Here are some things to remember when building relationships with families:

- Families of children with exceptionalities are used to having to advocate for their child.
- Families know their child best and may see strengths and needs that EAs and teachers miss.
- Families want their child to belong.
- Families can speak for a child who can't do so.
- Some families may have had bad experiences in their own school lives, or at other schools, that cause them to mistrust the school.
- Newcomer families may be unsure of their role with respect to the school.

You may need to be sensitive to and learn about cultures, language, religions, gender expressions, sexual orientations, and life experiences that are different from your own. This will help you to better understand the children you work with. It will also help the families learn to trust and be comfortable with you and the school.

## Relationships in Interdisciplinary Teams

You will be working as part of an interdisciplinary team that may include:

- Families
- Teachers
- Other EAs
- A principal
- Speech therapists
- Occupational therapists
- Other healthcare professionals
- Consultants
- Social workers
- Community liaison workers

Several of these individuals may be working with a particular child at a given time. Again, strong and clear communication is essential to a healthy and effective team. It is very important that all members of the team share information and work collaboratively.

All students will benefit when the individuals involved with them are working cohesively as a team. In Chapter 7 you will learn about the key role of communication in building relationships, along with strategies for communicating effectively.

 ## Takeaways

- EAs will be called upon to work with many different people in the course of a day.
- The ability to build positive relationships with students, teachers, families, colleagues, and other team members is one of the most important keys to success as an EA.

 ## Reflection and Discussion

- Imagine that you have been assigned to work with a teacher who seems unfriendly and gives you little direction. What do you think might be going on for them? What are some ways you could show them that you could be of help to them?
- You have been assigned to provide one-on-one support to a student who is frequently hospitalized with a serious and chronic health condition. What other persons or professions might be part of the interdisciplinary team that is supporting and/or working with this child?
- What strengths and challenges do you feel you would bring to working as part of an interdisciplinary team?

# 7

# Communication in Relationships

*Listen with curiosity. Speak with honesty. Act with
integrity. The greatest problem with communication
is we don't listen to understand. We listen to reply.
When we listen with curiosity, we don't listen with the
intent to reply. We listen for what's behind the words.*

—ROY T. BENNETT

## Learning Outcomes

After reading this chapter, you will be able to answer these questions:

- What is the role of communication in forming and maintaining relationships?
- What are some ways to become more effective as a listener?
- What is the best way to approach a situation where someone has very strong emotions?
- How should we respond to cultural differences in communication styles?
- What is *third-space dialogue* and how does it work?
- What is the best way to respond when children ask us if we like their work?

## Introduction

In Chapter 6, we talked about the web of relationships that you, as an EA, will navigate. Even if you are assigned to support only one child, your work still involves building relationships with the child, their teacher, and their family; with your colleagues; with consultants; with the child's classmates. You are in a unique position as a communicator: you are a "connector" between all of these people.

This chapter will illustrate the importance of effective communication skills in building relationships with others. It will help you understand the process of communication and become more effective with listening, sending messages, finding agreement when there are opposing perspectives, and responding children's efforts to communicate.

## The Role of Communication in Relationships

In early 2020, the COVID-19 virus entered Canada. To contain the spread of the virus, Canadians were asked to practice physical distancing. During this time, there was limited opportunity to talk face-to-face with our friends, family, and colleagues. We turned to social media to keep in touch, posting jokes, exchanging news, suggesting links to interesting websites. We hosted virtual meetings, had virtual parties, and went on virtual shopping trips with friends.

The degree of isolation was unprecedented, and the fact that we found creative ways to maintain connections shows the critical role that communication plays in building and sustaining relationships.

## What Is Communication?

On the surface, the act of communication is very simple: a message is sent and a message is received. What complicates the process is the filter of prior experiences and preconceptions that the message passes through between the sender and the receiver.

See what happens, for example, when Michael tells Carlos that his family has a new dog.

Michael                              Carlos

FIGURE 7.1. Communication misstep

Until Michael and Carlos communicate more fully, the picture that Carlos has of Michael's dog might be quite different from the one Michael is trying to convey. In fact, because they are two different people with two different sets of experiences, Michael will never be able to fully convey his meaning to Carlos exactly as he conceives it. Often, what the receiver understands isn't exactly what the sender is trying to communicate:

**FIGURE 7.2. Communication gap**

The goal in communication is to narrow the gap between what is sent and what is received in order to arrive at a shared meaning.

The example with Michael and Carlos focuses on the words they are saying. However, words are only a small part of a holistic view of communication. Perhaps Michael gestures with his hands to show that his dog is very small; that would certainly influence Carlos's interpretation of Michael's message. Maybe Michael uses a certain tone of voice when he is describing this new, tiny puppy: more information for Carlos to process. Recognizing the nonverbal cues that Michael is sending would help Carlos interpret his verbal message more accurately.

## Nonverbal Communication

As an EA, you may be working with individuals whose primary mode of communication is nonverbal, or who speak a language that you don't understand.

*Nonverbal communication* is the transmission of meaning without the use of words. In fact, in any interaction, only a small part of our communication is verbal. Psychologist Albert Mehrabian (1972/2017), who is widely known for his work with communication theory, estimated that communication is only about 7% verbal; meaning is mostly communicated through tone of voice (38%) and nonverbal cues (55%).

We communicate nonverbally through dress and physical appearance, posture and physical bearing, body position, touch, gesture, facial expression, and the way we use our time. We also communicate through our tone of voice and other nonverbal elements of verbal communication: volume, variety and expressiveness, rate, and rhythm.

Nonverbal cues help us to understand the verbal part of the communication, and most of us are already quite proficient at reading these cues.

Still, nonverbal communication can be a little more challenging when our conversation partner has a different style of communication—for example, if she or he is from a culture that is unfamiliar to us.

## Cultural Differences in Communication Style

Different cultures have distinctive ways of communicating. Some of the elements of communication that may vary across cultures are:

- Amount of eye contact
- Use of silence in conversation
- Direct or indirect approach to important topics
- Personal distance
- Use of titles or names in addressing one another
- Amount and kinds of touch
- Time spent getting acquainted versus getting to the point
- Amount of talk expected
- Amount and kinds of physical touch expected
- Acceptable and taboo subjects
- Use of humour
- Tone of voice
- Types of greetings
- Posture
- Use of gestures
- Amount and nature of self-disclosure

How do we respond to these differences, given that very few of us are experts in cross-cultural communication? How can we avoid communicating inappropriately or offensively? One thing we can do is to expect that there will be differences. If we expect differences, we will be more purposefully aware of what we are saying and doing. We will pay attention to how the other person might perceive the situation and make the adjustments necessary for successful communication. We will avoid interpreting the other person's speech and behaviour from our own frame of reference and try to understand it from their perspective. We will allow time for clarification and questions.

## The Importance of Active Listening

The most important skill for building satisfying relationships is listening. Everyone feels a need to be heard and understood, and this validation is particularly important for children. Active listening tells them that we genuinely want to know what they are thinking and how they are feeling. It tells them that they matter to us. The ability to relax, slow down, and really listen to what children are trying to say or to tell us with their actions is a gift we can give to the children we work with as EAs.

## What Is Active Listening?

*Active listening* is a listening technique that focuses on understanding where the other person is coming from rather than on responding. To see the power of active listening, consider the story of Asha, Maria, and the lost picture:

> Asha, a grade 1 student, is crying when she comes in from recess. Maria, an EA, notices her distress. She approaches Asha, kneels to be at her level, and looks at her face with a questioning expression.
>
> "I had my picture in my pocket and now it's gone," Asha sobs. Maria nods sympathetically and puts her hand gently on Asha's shoulder. "Somebody took it," Asha continues.
>
> At this point, Maria might be tempted to suggest that Asha might have lost it in the playground. Instead she responds to Asha's distress by tentatively naming her feelings.
>
> "It seems like you're pretty sad about losing your picture, aren't you?" Maria asks.
>
> "My daddy gave it to me last night!" Asha wails.
>
> Maria continues to focus on Asha's feelings. "It's so disappointing, isn't it!" Maria exclaims.
>
> Asha stops crying. "I think it fell out when I was playing with Elijah," she says.
>
> "Okay, let's go and look for it," says Maria.

What happened here to take Asha from the depths of despair to the point where she could problem-solve about her lost picture?

First of all, Maria showed her that she understood Asha's feelings. She connected with Asha with her body language (kneeling to her level, a questioning look, a sympathetic nod, a hand on her shoulder). She also used a tone of voice that echoed Asha's emotions when she said, "It's so disappointing!"

Maria genuinely felt Asha's distress. Her attentiveness encouraged Asha to tell why the picture was so important to her. It would have been tempting to suggest a solution to Asha's problem, but Maria also knew that there was no point in trying to deal with the problem when strong feelings would get in the way. Attempting to cheer Asha up, criticizing her for being careless, challenging her assumption that the picture was stolen, or questioning her about where she might have lost it would not respond to the message Asha was sending: the message that she was heartbroken about losing the picture her daddy had given her. Instead, she felt understood, and this freed her to think constructively about how she might have lost the picture.

It's important to notice, too, that through listening actively, Maria left space for Asha to solve her own problem. In doing so, she was fostering Asha's independence, competency, and resiliency.

Active listening is a skill that you can learn and improve with practice. Let's look at some of the aspects of active listening that Maria demonstrated.

## Genuine Attention and Concern

Active listening is a technique that grows from an attitude of genuine concern. This concern is conveyed in both verbal and non-verbal ways.

**What Do You Think?**

What verbal and nonverbal ways did Maria use to convey her caring to Asha?

## Arriving at Shared Meaning

The goal of active listening is to arrive at a shared meaning—that is, the point at which the speaker can honestly say, "Yes, that's what I mean." Maria knew that Asha had reached that point when she switched from expressing her disappointment to figuring out how to solve the problem.

The underlying premise of active listening is that the speaker is the expert on his or her own experience; the listener, on the other hand, is guessing whether or not he or she is interpreting the speaker's message correctly. For that reason, it's important that the listener use a tentative, questioning style.

## Paraphrasing Feelings

Maria used an active listening strategy when she *paraphrased* Asha's emotions by putting them into words: "It seems like you're pretty sad about losing your picture, aren't you?"; "It's so disappointing, isn't it!" This raises another important point: Whenever you are dealing with a situation in which someone is feeling strong emotions, as Maria was in this situation, always respond to the emotions first. Until the emotions have been acknowledged, the person won't be able to move on.

## Paraphrasing Content

Active listening can also include paraphrasing the content of a message by putting it into your own words to make sure you are understanding its meaning. A paraphrase might begin with, "Do you mean…?" or "It sounds like you…" or "What I'm understanding is…". It goes on to summarize the content of the speaker's message in a tentative manner, ending in a questioning tone phrase such as, "Am I right?" or "Is that true?" Paraphrasing is especially useful when you are listening to a complaint, trying to understand new information, or trying to solve a problem.

Here's an example:

> **Tazim:** *Yesterday I had to go to violin lessons right after school and then we went out to eat and then I had baseball practice. When I came home, I wanted to do my homework but my mom said it was time for bed.*
>
> **You:** *Are you saying that you were too busy to do your homework, then?*

## Open-Ended Questions

You can also use open-ended questions to encourage students to elaborate or problem-solve. Open-ended questions are questions that require more than a yes or no answer. For example, "Can you tell me more about…?" or "How did you do that?" If Asha hadn't come to a solution on her own, Maria might have asked, "What could we do about this?" or "How do you think we should go about looking for your picture?"

## Third-Space Dialogue

Active listening allows you to create a *third-space dialogue*. A third-space dialogue creates a conversational space between two people that is not about one or the other but about the meanings they co-create together. Third-space dialogue is an especially effective way to communicate across cultures, but is not exclusively a cross-cultural approach. The dialogue begins with a genuine desire to learn about and honour the perspective of the other. It requires that the conversational partners interact as equals who are committed to finding common ground. It tries to set aside issues of power, authority, status, and age difference. It avoids judgements as well as proposing solutions before fully exploring feelings, possibilities, and points of view.

Active listening is central to third-space dialogue. In third-space dialogue, active listening is taken to the point at which each participant can honestly say, "If I were in your situation, I might feel the same way."

> When Henry's mother, Carmen, approaches Greg, an EA, she is visibly upset. She complains to Greg that Henry is bringing quite a lot of his lunch home after school. Greg listens attentively as she tells him that Henry was very small when he was born and she was afraid he would die. She tells him how she has encouraged him to eat from the time he was little. He has been ill a lot and she worries that when he doesn't eat, he might get sick. Greg actively listens: He asks a couple of questions to clarify Carmen's meaning, and paraphrases some of what she says to make sure he understands.
>
> Greg reaches a point where he can genuinely sympathize with Carmen. He thinks that if he were her, he might feel the same way. When he believes that Carmen has expressed her fears fully, he feels he can introduce his own perspectives. He tells her that Henry is often in a hurry to get out to play and perhaps he doesn't want to take the time to finish his lunch. He also tactfully suggests that Henry's lunches are quite large and wonders if they might be more than Henry wants or can eat.
>
> "Let's decide on the best way to handle this," Greg proposes and Carmen nods.
>
> "I guess I do pack him pretty big lunches," she says.
>
> "I wonder if we might be able to have him start his lunch just a bit earlier, so he'll have more time to finish before recess," Greg adds.
>
> They discuss a little longer and come up with a plan. Carmen will monitor Henry's real lunch needs and Greg will look for a way to give him more time to eat. They agree to check in again in two weeks to see if Henry is eating well and has enough energy on this new plan.

In the example above, Greg listens carefully and actively to let Carmen fully express her concerns. Only when she has done so to the extent that he can understand and empathize does he put forth his own point of view. From there, they are able to move to problem-solving together.

There are two sides to any communicative relationship, however: listening to the messages you are being sent, but also *sending* messages yourself. There are skills for being an effective sender just as there are for being a good listener.

## Being a Responsible Sender

The skills of a responsible, effective sender include:

- Being aware of your thoughts, feelings, intentions, and behaviours
- Ensuring that it's a good time to talk
- Using "I" language; avoiding speaking for others
- Allowing time for the listener to respond
- Checking for shared meaning
- Staying with the conversation until you both feel satisfied that it's complete

## Avoiding Roadblocks

*Roadblocks* are statements that shut down communication. When communicating with children, roadblocks are adult-directed and don't help children to develop the skills they need to deal with problems or regulate their behaviour. These roadblocks include responses that criticize, shame, explicitly direct, moralize, kid or joke, avoid or prematurely solve the problem at hand, interpret the reasons behind the problem, or directly question the child about why the problem has occurred. Even misplaced praise can have a negative impact: How would you feel if you came to someone with a concern and they dismissed it with, "You're so smart, I'm sure you'll be able to handle it"?

 **What Do You Think?**

Imagine that Salwa has lost her gloves for the third time this month. When she tells Angela, her EA, Angela responds in one of the following ways:

- *Criticizing*: "You've lost your gloves three times this month. Why can't you keep track of your belongings?"
- *Shaming*: "Your parents work hard to buy your clothes! Now you've lost your gloves again?"
- *Directing*: "Go out to where you were in the playground and look around for them."
- *Solving the problem*: "I think there are some gloves in the Lost and Found that you could use."
- *Moralizing*: "People need to be responsible if they're going to succeed in the world."
- *Avoiding the problem*: "What did you think about the way the game turned out?"
- *Kidding*: "You have the record for losing gloves, Salwa!"

- *Interpreting*: "I think the reason you lose your gloves is that you take them off, put them in your pocket, and they fall out."
- *Questioning*: "Why do you think you lose your gloves so often?"

How do you think Salwa will feel and/or react to each of these responses? How might she react if Angela says, "You seem to be pretty upset about losing your gloves," instead?

In the next chapter, we'll consider some of the research that reflects the importance of relationships in fostering children's healthy development.

 ## Takeaways

- Communication—verbal and nonverbal—is the key to forming healthy, effective relationships.
- Effective communication occurs when the message the sender sends and the message the receiver receives are as similar as possible.
- We need to be aware that there are cultural elements in communication and be open to the possibility of differences in communication styles.
- Third-space dialogue is an effective way to resolve opposing viewpoints, particularly when there are cultural differences.
- We can learn strategies to make our communication more effective. Improving communication skills takes awareness and practice.
- The way we respond to children's efforts will either encourage or discourage their further initiative and independence.

 ## Reflection and Discussion

- Imagine that your partner or roommate has come home very upset because of unfair treatment at work. What would your conversation with them look like? What are some of the principles you would want to remember when responding?
- The grade 11 choir is planning a two-day tour to a nearby city. A parent who is new to Canada approaches you on the playground to express his surprise that the students will be away overnight and to say that his daughter won't be coming along. You know that his daughter has been counting on this trip; moreover, she has a beautiful voice and will be a real loss to the choir. You want to understand why he is so opposed to her coming on the trip. Imagine a third-space dialogue that would allow you to hear his concerns, to express yours, and to arrive at a mutual understanding.

# What Do Children Need to Succeed?

*Treat people as if they were what they ought to be and you help them become what they are capable of being.*

—*JOHANN W. VAN GOETHE*

## Learning Outcomes

After reading this chapter, you will be able to answer these questions:

- What are the implications of brain research for EAs' work with students?
- What is resilience and why is it important?
- How can we support students in developing resilience?
- Why is it a problem to use a single measure of intelligence to measure the intelligence of all students?
- How can labelling limit students' growth?
- What are some of the characteristics of a healthy self-esteem?
- What are some of the things we can do to help children build a healthy self-esteem?

## Introduction

This chapter briefly summarizes research and theory about the kinds of environment and support that children need to facilitate their healthy development. Brain research, investigations of resiliency, and theories of intelligence and self-esteem indicate the importance of a supportive learning environment that takes into account the whole range of human needs and abilities.

# The Developing Brain

What makes us grow into the people we are? Why are some able to bounce back from tragic events while others never recover? Why are some of us more likely than others to develop addictions, depression, or heart disease?

For many years, people have debated about the relative influence of nature (biological factors such as our genes) and nurture (the social and cultural factors of the environment in which we grow). Research on the developing brain has settled that debate by showing us that nature and nurture are intertwined from the very beginning of life. Genes determine when certain brain circuits get built, but experiences determine how.

Interactions with parents or caregivers are key to the growth of brain circuitry. Positive, nurturing interactions build strong brain circuits while threatening ones weaken circuits (Pfitzer, 2020). These foundations are laid in the early years of life. While brains can be changed and strengthened later in life, making these changes becomes progressively more difficult.

## Developmental Risk Factors

Factors that threaten healthy brain development are both biological and environmental. You'll notice that trauma, while environmental, has a separate category because of its profound influence on children's behaviour and learning (Kaiser, 2020).

### Biological risk factors

- Temperament
- Genes
- Complications of pregnancy and birth
- Substance abuse during pregnancy
- Neurological delays
- Emotional and behavioural disorders
- Gender
- Serious medical conditions

### Environmental risk factors

- Family factors and parenting style
  › Abuse, neglect, domestic violence

› Loss of a loved one

› Harsh parenting style

› Parents suffering from mental illness, addictions

- Poverty and the social conditions surrounding it

› Poor nutrition, housing, and/or medical care

### Trauma

- Displacement or refugee trauma

› Not being part of the mainstream culture or language

- School or community violence

› Being bullied or rejected

- Natural tragedies

› Natural disasters, pandemics

- Intergenerational trauma

› Impact of residential schools

## The Effects of Stress and Trauma

This book was written in the midst of the COVID-19 pandemic. As we write, schools and childcare centres are closed, people are asked to stay at home, businesses are shuttered, travel is limited, people are dying, and healthcare professionals and resources are stretched to the limit. This is incredibly stressful in its own right. The pandemic is also predicted to result in a long-lasting economic depression with high rates of unemployment, which will result in persistent financial challenges for many families. It's a stressful period for everyone, and one that prompts us to ask what the long-term effects of this and other stressful events and circumstances might be on children's brains and functioning.

Research tells us that toxic stress or traumatic events alter brain architecture in ways that prevent social, emotional and cognitive competencies from developing to their full genetic potential. Stressful situations cause the adrenal gland to release the hormone cortisol. Where stress is extreme or long term, the excess cortisol can affect the hippocampus, a part of the brain that is responsible for converting short-term memories into long-term memories (Kaiser, 2020; Centre on the Developing Child, 2020; Pickens & Tschlopp, 2017). We call the psychological effects of severe and/or long-term stress *trauma*.

Not all stress is toxic. If stress is mild or brief, a supportive adult can help a child get through it without long-term effects. More severe stress and trauma does have the potential to harm and requires supportive adults to moderate the effects.

In your work as an EA, you will encounter many children who live with the effects of stress, whether the causes are biological or environmental. Children who live with abuse or domestic violence, children who are adapting to a new culture, children who are poor or homeless, and children who are socially isolated are among those whose ability to learn may be limited by the effects of stress and trauma. Director of the Yale Center for Emotional Intelligence, Marc Brackett (as cited in Kahn, 2013), reminds us:

> Something we now know, from doing dozens of studies, is that emotions can either enhance or hinder your ability to learn. They affect our attention and our memory. If you're very anxious about something, or agitated, how well can you focus on what's being taught? (para. 12)

Their traumatic experiences have some children feeling profoundly unsafe and unable to trust. They may react with challenging behaviours or

**TABLE 8.1. Some Effects of Trauma**

| | |
|---|---|
| **Intellectual** | • Difficulty thinking, learning, and concentrating<br>• Impaired memory<br>• Difficulty switching from one thought or activity to another |
| **Emotional** | • Low self-esteem<br>• Feeling unsafe<br>• Inability to regulate emotions<br>• Difficulty forming attachments to caregivers<br>• Trouble with friendships<br>• Trust issues<br>• Depression and/or anxiety |
| **Physical** | • Inability to control physical responses to stress<br>• Chronic illness, even into adulthood (heart disease, obesity) |
| **Behavioural** | • Lack of impulse control<br>• Distrusting or disobeying adults<br>• Fighting<br>• Aggression<br>• Running away<br>• Dissociating (feeling disconnected from reality)<br>• Substance abuse<br>• Suicide |

*Note.* Table adapted from Child Welfare Information Gateway, 2014.

by withdrawing. Realizing that difficult behaviours can have roots in stress or trauma can help you avoid taking them personally so that you can offer a calm, reassuring response.

Trauma, whether it be from a single event or long-term stress that spans days, years, or even generations, can affect every aspect of a child's intellectual, emotional, physical, and behavioural development.

## Secondary Traumatic Stress (STS) and Intergenerational Trauma

Trauma may be a response to a recent event, but it can also show itself as *secondary traumatic stress* (STS) or *intergenerational trauma*.

STS affects children or adults who have experienced traumatic life events in the past. These individuals may feel particularly unsafe in the face of a new threat. The new threat may trigger feelings from the previous trauma. Compassion fatigue, described as emotional and physical exhaustion incurred by caring for others, is related to STS.

*Intergenerational trauma* refers to the effects of trauma that can be passed on through generations. Persons who are closely connected to those who have experienced trauma may adopt their ways of coping. In many Indigenous communities in Canada, for example, high levels of suicide, substance abuse, and mental health issues are linked to past and present experiences of colonialism (Poole, Talbot & Nathoo, 2017).

# Building Resiliency

Resiliency has to do with our ability to adapt positively and quickly in the face of adversity. Michael Unger (2014) and his colleagues have studied how educational institutions can build on strengths, develop pathways to resilience, and enable families and communities to access the resources they need. They have found that schools can promote resilience by:

- Developing positive relationships with students by caring, actively listening, and being available to them
- Taking steps to end bullying and harassment at school
- Taking responsibility for ensuring that students are successful at school
- Helping students who need assistance to access the supports they need
- Showing empathy for students' adversity and providing positive strategies for dealing with it

Trauma-informed classrooms, a classroom model discussed below, put these ideas, along with what we know about trauma, into practice to create safe, nurturing environments.

## Trauma-Informed Classrooms

*Trauma-informed* classrooms recognize the possibility of stress and trauma among students and work to help them function well and develop resiliency.

Trauma-informed classrooms and the teachers and EAs that create them:

- Give students a place where they can feel physically and emotionally safe
- Establish predictability; have a schedule and prepare students for transitions
- Build a sense of trust by following through with promises and being transparent with explanations
- Offer choices so that children can have a sense of control over their lives
- Don't punish children or give them timeouts for their challenging behaviour. Punishment models the use of power to control others, while time away and timeouts may be perceived as rejection
- Teach problem-solving and stress management skills
- Model a healthy response to stressful events, including being in control of one's own feelings, and accepting and reflecting the feelings of children (Kaiser, 2020; Pickens & Tschlopp, 2017)

The conditions in these classrooms can help all children, not just children experiencing the effects of trauma, thrive.

In the next section, we turn from the discussion of resiliency to look at the impact that intelligence testing has had over the years and some other ways that we can consider intelligence.

## Views of Intelligence

Intelligence tests (IQ tests) were developed over 100 years ago and have since seen many uses, both good (e.g., identifying students who might need extra help in school) and bad (e.g., as a basis for forced sterilization). Intelligence is highly prized in our society, but the possibility of distilling intelligence into one numerical score is highly problematic. Even Albert Binet, the inventor of the first intelligence test, warned that intelligence is influenced by a number of factors. He noted that intelligence changes over time, that the intelligence test does not measure creativity or emotional intelligence, and that intelligences can only be compared among individuals from similar backgrounds (Martschenko, 2018).

## What Do You Think?

> Lindsey and Cinzia had been best friends from their first days
> of kindergarten. In the fall, just as they were about to begin
> high school and brimming with anticipation, they found
> online IQ tests and each completed one. The results shocked
> them. While Lindsey scored 120, Cinzia tested at 85! How
> could this be, when they had achieved rather equally so far
> throughout school?
>
> They began high school together. They both struggled
> with the new, bigger environment. In the end, though,
> Lindsey finished grade 12 and went on to university. Cinzia
> dropped out of school after grade 10, convinced that she
> was "too dumb" to complete. Later in life, Cinzia went back to
> school and eventually completed a nursing degree.

What factors may have influenced the difference in scores between the two
friends? How did Cinzia's score affect her attitude towards school? Given how
the story ends, do you think the scores from the IQ test accurately reflected the
friends' intelligences?

## Multiple Intelligences

Howard Gardener (1993) challenged this one-dimensional view of intelligence by developing a theory of multiple intelligences. He believes that we
are all intelligent, but in different ways. Gardener identified eight kinds of
intelligences, each of which has implications for teaching and learning:

1. *Linguistic intelligence* is the capacity to work with words, orally and
   in writing. Students who have high linguistic intelligence do well with
   traditional methods of school. They enjoy tasks that involve reading,
   writing, research, and wordplay.

2. *Logical-mathematical intelligence* refers to the ability to use numbers
   effectively and reason well. Students with logical-mathematical intelligence enjoy activities such as puzzles, mazes, calculations, and codes.

3. *Musical intelligence* refers to the ability to recognize and create music.
   Students with a high degree of musical intelligence like to express
   their thoughts and emotions through instruments, singing, choral
   readings, raps, or jingles.

4. *Spatial intelligence* has to do with sensitivity to form, shape, colour, line, and space, as well as the ability to visualize an object or create mental pictures. These students enjoy tasks where they can represent their learning visually, as in models or maps.

5. *Bodily-kinesthetic intelligence* refers to the ability to express oneself using movements and gestures. Activities might include sports, games, dance, field trips, acting out a story, or roleplaying.

6. *Interpersonal intelligence* is the ability to relate to and understand others. Students with interpersonal intelligence learn well through group projects and tasks, debates, interviews, and discussions.

7. *Intrapersonal intelligence* means being able to understand one's inner self and use that information effectively in one's own life. Journaling, goal setting, poetry, and meditation fit well with this type of intelligence.

8. *Naturalistic intelligence* refers to knowledge of, and respect for, the natural world. Students with naturalistic intelligence thrive on outdoor activities such as nature walks, exploring, and collecting and identifying plants and animals.

If there are so many different ways to be intelligent, it is clear that a single measure of intelligence will be insufficient to give us an accurate account of the intelligence of any individual. When we discuss differentiating instruction in Chapter 9, you will begin to see ways to adapt content to best meet the needs of children with various intelligences and learning styles.

## Beginning with Strengths

How we think about and describe a student makes a big difference in the opportunities we provide for them. Think about the following examples.

> Student A is a 15-year-old female who is developmentally delayed and low-achieving. She is unable to read beyond a grade 2 level, is lazy about completing assignments, and is sometimes aggressive with classmates. She dresses sloppily and has unkempt hair.
>
> Student B is a 15-year-old female who has a profound love for music and is able to learn best when concepts are presented in rhythms, songs, or choral readings. In younger grades, she was subject to bullying by classmates, but she has learned to assert herself when she perceives that she is being

> treated unfairly. She is concerned about the environment so favours thrift-store clothing that she assembles in creative ways.

Based on the descriptions, what would you expect of these two students in terms of their behaviour and performance in school? If you were asked to make predictions about the future of Student A and Student B, what would you anticipate?

Student A doesn't seem to have a lot going for her. She is described as having low cognitive ability, poor study habits, poor social skills, and an untidy physical presentation. Student B, however, is musically gifted, assertive, socially conscious, and creative. These are traits that could take her far.

This brings us to the punch line: students A and B are the same person, seen through two different lenses. The first focuses on what she is not able to do while the second shows what she can do. The second description comes from someone who knows her well enough to see her talents, passions, and potential. This is the person who will be able to form a positive relationship with her, find the best ways to help her learn, and nourish her creativity.

Think about a child you know. How would you describe that child? Now look at your description and see if there are descriptors that could be phrased more positively. For example, a child who might be described as a daydreamer could also be described as imaginative, and a child who is labelled as having attention deficit disorder (ADD) could be described as a bodily-kinesthetic learner.

> **Say this:** Natalia has autism.
> **Not this:** Natalia is autistic / an autistic girl.
> **Say this:** The student who has Down syndrome.
> **Not this:** The Down syndrome student.
> **Say this:** A child who is blind.
> **Not this:** The blind child.

We assign labels to people and things as a kind of shorthand and a way of making sense of the world. Labels are necessary and convenient but, in labelling people, we run the risk of limiting their potential. If we have high expectations of someone rather than seeing them through the lens of their diagnosis, they are likely to see themselves as capable of achieving. We must always assume competence.

Consider, again, the child you know. Think about the labels that have been given that child—and now think beyond them. Even when they are accurate, they are only a small part of who the child is. When you are speaking of a child, always be sure that the child comes first.

## Understanding Self-Esteem

What is self-esteem? Defined very simply, self-esteem has to do with our opinion of ourselves. As opposed to *self-concept*, which is how we would describe ourselves ("I am a student"), *self-esteem* is about how we judge or evaluate ourselves ("I am a good student").

People with a healthy self-esteem have achieved a good balance of liking who they are and recognizing ways they can continue to grow. They feel worthy of being loved and accepted by others, so they are more likely to have fulfilling friendships and to commit to working through difficult interpersonal situations. They see problems and challenges as opportunities to grow, and don't feel diminished by failure. They are resilient—that is, they can quickly adapt to changes in their lives, even when these involve significant adversity or stress.

While biology has some influence on self-esteem development, it is generally accepted that the environment plays a larger role. Individuals with healthy self-esteem usually grew up in homes where parents were affectionate, responsive, and appreciative. In the words of one researcher, they "treat their children as though they matter" (Kaufman, 2017, para. 6). Self-esteem is enhanced when important adults and peers treat the child with respect, give them opportunities to make meaningful decisions and contributions, and demonstrate trust. They encourage children to set their own goals rather than measuring themselves and their achievements against others. These adults show the child that they are unconditionally worthy of love and acceptance.

Many of our communications with children are responses to work that they have done. As we see in the next section, these responses can either encourage or stifle children's further efforts.

## Encouraging Students' Efforts

The self-esteem movement of the 1960s and 1970s has been denounced for producing children, now adults, who have an inflated sense of their own abilities and worth. This came about because well-meaning families and school authorities used indiscriminate praise in hopes of raising children with high self-esteem.

But how *should* we respond when little Vashti brings us her drawing and asks, "Do you like my picture?" For many of us, the automatic response would be, "Oh yes, it's beautiful," or at least, "Nice." If we're busy, we might barely look at the picture before we move on to another child.

Giving a truly encouraging response, however, requires that we pay attention. Such a response shows Vashti that we take her work seriously. We might comment on aspects of her drawing—for example, the colours she used, the details she included, the lines and shapes in it. We might also notice the effort she put into it.

Let's consider how Vashti might think and feel about the two types of responses:

**TABLE 8.2. Praise Versus Encouragement**

| PRAISE | HOW VASHTI THINKS AND FEELS: |
|---|---|
| That's beautiful, Vashti. | • My EA likes my picture.<br>• Since my EA likes this one, I'll make another one like it.<br>• It's important that I please my EA. |
| **ENCOURAGEMENT** | **HOW VASHTI THINKS AND FEELS:** |
| Vashti, look at all the colours you use! (The EA points at and names the colours.) | I did use lots of colours! I'll try some other colours in my next picture. |
| I noticed you working carefully to get the circle and square about the same size. | I wanted to get the square and circle the same size and I think it worked. |
| I noticed that you worked on this picture for a long time. You added a lot of detail. (The EA points out some of the features.) | • When I work carefully, I get a result that I'm happy with.<br>• I'll try that in my other work. |
| Are you happy with how your picture turned out? | What matters is how I feel about my work. |

What do you notice about the difference between Vashti's interpretations of the two kinds of responses? You can see that praise sends the message that the outcome is what matters rather than the effort and thought that went into it. Praise also tells Vashti that the EA's approval is more important than her own satisfaction and evaluation. This dependence on adult approval tells her that she is only worthy when she pleases adults and causes her to constantly search for validation. It also makes it likely that she will stick to her tried-and-true formula in her next picture rather than branching out into new colours and new techniques.

While praise teaches children to rely on external validation, encouragement teaches children to look inside themselves for answers, motivation, purpose, and direction.

Psychologist Carol Dweck (2006) was one of the first to show how praise can impede learning. She was interested in students' attitudes about failure and found that when students believe they can get smarter by putting in extra time and effort, they were able to achieve more. In a widely cited quote, Dweck advises:

> If parents want to give their children a gift, the best thing they can do is to teach their children to love challenges, be intrigued by mistakes, enjoy effort and keep on learning. That way, their children don't have to be slaves of praise. They will have a lifelong way to build and repair their own confidence. (176–77)

Research tells us that children need supportive environments, caring mentors, and skillful instruction in order to thrive. In Chapter 9, we will consider universal design for learning (UDL), an approach that is intended to provide support and access to all students.

## Takeaways

- Brain research tells us that emotions affect our ability to learn.
- Resiliency theory reminds us of the value of positive relationships.
- The idea of multiple intelligences expands our concept of human potential.
- The labels we use, and the way we describe people, can make a difference in the expectations that we have for them.
- Self-esteem theory reinforces the importance of feeling valued and capable and having a sense of belonging.
- How we describe and label students affects the experiences we are likely to provide for them. We have to ensure that we aren't using labels that limit their possibilities.
- How we respond to children's efforts can teach them to explore and learn (encouragement) or focus their efforts on trying to please us (praise).

## Reflection and Discussion

- Think about times when you have been given direct or indirect messages about your capabilities in various areas. How have these messages influenced you? Are there things that you would like to try but have avoided because you thought you might fail?

# Universal Design for
# Learning (UDL)

*Every student can learn, just not on the
same day, or in the same way.*

—GEORGE EVANS

## Learning Outcomes

After reading this chapter, you will be able to answer these questions:

- How would you explain universal design for learning (UDL)?
- What are some of the characteristics of a UDL classroom?
- What are some strategies for differentiating instruction?
- What does it mean to accommodate and adapt instruction and modify curriculum?
- How might we construct an individualized learning plan?
- How can technologies be used to assist children with exceptionalities?
- What can EAs do to support learning in a UDL classroom?
- How can you support the specific learning needs of children who have particular exceptionalities?

## Introduction

This chapter will introduce you to the concept of universal design for learning (UDL), an approach for meeting children's diverse needs within an inclusive classroom. From there, we will look at the characteristics of a UDL classroom, and how teachers and EAs can plan and work with individual students in such a classroom.

## Stories of Diverse Learners

> Romy is struggling to understand the expectations and
> assignments in her English class. She is embarrassed when
> Manuel, the EA, makes a point of specifically explaining class
> material to her as she doesn't want to stand out from her
> classmates. "I've got it, I've got it," she says. She appears to
> be dawdling for the rest of the class and it quickly becomes
> apparent that she still doesn't understand.

> Steven catches on quickly to the math assignment and knows
> that once it's finished he can pursue his real interest: a fantasy
> cartoon that he is creating. The assignment holds little inter-
> est for him, and he rushes to finish it.

> Nasima's family have recently arrived as refugees to Canada.
> English is very difficult for her. She works hard but nonethe-
> less struggles to understand the assignments in her classes.
> She is also facing difficulties at home, where her family mem-
> bers depend on her to help them understand and cope with
> their new environment.

These students are just three in a class of 30 students with varied learning and social needs who are part of an inclusive grade 10 English class.
They represent only a small part of the diversity that you will encounter in
classrooms, but even in this classroom we can begin to see the breadth of
different challenges, strengths, and learning styles that could exist within a
single classroom.

UDL is a teaching and learning approach intended to meet the diverse
needs of students in any classroom you may encounter.

## What Is UDL?

*Universal design for learning* (UDL) has to do with removing barriers to
learning in order to make it accessible to all students. The goal is to provide
equal opportunities for each student. The concept of UDL stems from the

concept of universal design in architecture, which works to make buildings that are accessible to people of all abilities.

UDL is a concept that encompasses social-emotional, instructional, and structural aspects of learning. It is strengths-based, using curriculum design and technologies in order to build on the strengths of students. UDL can involve:

- Using multiple ways to present content such as audio, video, roleplays, or other hands-on experiences
- Offering multiple ways to show mastery of the content such as paper tests, presentations, projects, and artistic representations
- Using various ways to motivate and engage students such as games, gaming, or simulations
- Using individualized or specialized supports that relate to the learning needs of individual students such as alternative and augmentative communication systems, sign language interpreters, or mental health support

## School-Wide UDL

UDL works best when it is embraced throughout a school. The school can work to create an environment where all students feel welcomed and valued, and where they all have access to facilities and activities. In this environment, teachers and EAs will receive the support and resources they need to implement UDL in the classroom and in working with individual children.

## The UDL Classroom

If we look into a UDL classroom, we might see something like this:

> Students in the grade 4 classroom are learning about how plants disperse seeds. Some of the students are looking up methods of dispersal online and jotting down a few notes for the movie they are making. Two students are making a poster about how carnivorous plants disperse seeds. Others are making 3-dimensional sculptures of seeds. Several are gluing different kinds of seeds onto a poster. One child is working with an EA to find all the books about plants and seeds in the classroom library. While all the students are participating in the study of seed dispersal, each child is able to bring their own skills and interests to the lesson and can participate at their own level.

In a UDL classroom:

- The environment is comfortable and inviting.
  - › Furniture is arranged so that students can choose the workspace that is best for them.
  - › The various cultures and abilities of children in the room are represented in pictures and artifacts.
- The teachers and EAs know each student well, and their individual strengths and challenges.
  - › They work with the students to set specific goals for their learning.
  - › Students receive regular feedback that helps them reflect on their progress and determine new goals and strategies.
- The environment is respectful and students are comfortable asking for help when they need it.
- The classroom has set routines and conveys high expectations.
- The students are grouped according to their interests and learning strengths.
  - › These groups change with different tasks, depending on students' interests, strengths, and challenges in different areas.
- Content is provided in various formats such as paper and digital books, images or charts, videos, learning games, music, or text-to-speech.
- Information is adapted for student understanding (e.g., materials are given in their first language).
- There are multiple options for expressing ideas and presenting assignments.
  - › These might include doing a group presentation, drawing a comic strip, building a model, or completing a test in digital format or with audio questions.
- Students have access to learning software, which can be navigated and controlled in various ways.

UDL may be implemented through a variety of intersecting methods, including differentiated instruction (DI), tiered instruction, scaffolding, and individual education plans (IEPs).

## Differentiated Instruction (DI)

Universal design for learning means that children are taught in a way that accommodates their learning style and needs. When teachers make decisions about how they will teach based on the individual strengths, experiences, abilities, and needs of each student, they are *differentiating instruction*. Generally speaking, these decisions can involve differentiating the learning environment, content, process, and product of a lesson or project (Tomlinson, 2000). These differentiations may take the form of accommodations, adaptations, modifications, or alternative expectations.

## Differentiating What?[4]

### Learning environment

Differentiating the learning environment may involve:

- Providing quiet workspaces in the room free of distractions
- Organizing places that provide for student collaboration
- Providing materials that reflect a variety of home settings and cultures
- Developing routines for students to access help when the teacher is not available
- Organizing the environment for student movement (as some learners need to move around to learn)
- Giving students choice over where and how they learn best (e.g., individually, in a quiet location away from others, in an active area of the room, as part of a group)

### Content

Differentiating the content of a lesson may involve:

- Providing reading materials at varying readability levels
- Presenting ideas through auditory and visual means
- Providing mini-lessons for small groups to reteach an idea or skill
- Using classroom "experts"—students who understand a concept well—to reteach it to others who are still in the learning phase
- Allowing students to work at the edge of their readiness level

### Process

Differentiating the process of a lesson may involve:

- Using tiered instruction/activities in which all learners work on the same content and skills but use different levels of support, challenge, or complexity (See "Tiered Instruction" below)
- Creating interest centres that encourage student exploration of topics of interest

---

[4] Information in this section is adapted from Tomlinson, 2000.

- Setting up a personalized student task folder containing common classroom assignments and specific individualized work
- Utilizing manipulatives or other hands-on activities to support learning
- Using drawings, diagrams, and charts to aid understanding
- Using headings to organize information
- Adjusting the length of time students are given to complete a task
- Using meaningful, engaging, relevant, and age-appropriate tasks
- Beginning from what students already know/can do, and teaching from there

### Product

Differentiating the product of a lesson or project may involve:

- Allowing students to choose how they wish to demonstrate their learning (art project, oral PowerPoint presentation, puppet show, role-playing, etc.)
- Giving students the option to work alone or in groups on their product
- Providing students the option to design their own product to meet assignment requirements

## Differentiating How?[5]

Decisions about learning environment, content, product, and process will take into consideration the strengths and learning needs of the student. When you are working as an EA, you will hear the terms *accommodations, adaptations, modifications* and *alternate expectations*. It is important that you understand the meaning of each of these terms.

- *Accommodations.* Making changes to the way a student accesses information and demonstrates learning
  - › Examples: recording teacher presentations, using speech-to-text apps, giving additional time for completing tasks, using an electronic device rather than a pencil
- *Adaptations.* Making changes to the method of instruction
  - › Examples: using a calculator for a math test, offering a word-bank of choices, using visual cues and prompts, providing Braille books, or providing translations into other languages

---

[5] Information in this section is adapted from Tomlinson, 2000.

- *Modifications.* Making changes to what a student is expected to learn (the curriculum)
  › Examples: if the class is practicing multiplication using three digits, a modified assignment could be matching numbers from 1 to 5 with corresponding objects; if the class is learning about the structures of local, provincial, and federal government, a modified assignment could be learning about the parts of their community.

- *Alternative expectations.* Changing what a student is expected to be able to do, with a view to accommodating skills that a student requires but that are not represented in the curriculum, such as mobility skills, social skills, or routines
  › Examples: learning to hang up their backpack and jacket, saying thank you or good morning, throwing a ball, taking turns, putting up their hand to speak, understanding how to respond during a fire drill

## Using Technology to Differentiate Instruction

Assistive technologies are making it possible for children with exceptionalities to be successful in school—and sometimes to become the "cool kid" with intriguing technological devices.

As outlined by Lynch (2018), assistive technologies fall into several categories:

- *Alternate input devices.* These devices allow students with disabilities to use computers and related technology. They include touch screens, onscreen keyboards, modified keyboards, sip-and-puff systems, and joysticks that can be operated with various body parts.
- *Sensory enhancers.* These include voice analyzers, augmentative communication tools and speech synthesizers.
- *Speech-to-text options.* These technologies can help students who are blind or who have mobility or dexterity problems. There are some that "talk back" to students and let them know about potential errors in their work.
- *Screen readers.* These technologies inform students about what is on a screen, including nonlinguistic elements.
- *Language acquisition through motor planning (LAMP).* LAMP technology is especially helpful for students who don't speak or have limited verbal skills. Students with autism and related disorders may use LAMP principles to communicate effectively.

Lynch (2018) points out that devices that aren't intended for children with exceptionalities can still be useful to them. Digital tablets have been found to be especially useful for students on the autism spectrum. Children with sight difficulties can benefit from e-readers, which allow students to change font size and brightness. Some even include speaking command options. Noise cancelling headphones are another useful technology that can help children focus.

While technology can be useful and fascinating, it's important to remember that technology is intended as a support rather than as an end in itself. Any technology used to assist a student with an individualized education plan (IEP, see page 91) should reflect that student's IEP and be geared to the needs and characteristics of the student.

EAs are invariably the persons responsible for setting up and understanding how these devices work and also for operating other technologies in the classroom. Learning how to use all kinds of classroom technologies increases your value as an EA.

## Tiered Instruction

*Tiered instruction* is a way of differentiating instruction so that each student can work at their own level. Children in the class all learn the same basic skills and concepts, but through varying methods. There are several different ways to do this:

- *Tiering by level*: using different books, asking different questions, using different activities and assignments, modifying lessons in various ways
- *Tiering by interest*: allowing an assignment to be completed in different ways depending on children's interests
- *Tiering by learning styles*: giving a variety of assignments that tap into different learning styles
- *Tiering by resources*: matching project materials to student readiness, like reading and comprehension level

In the grade 4 science class described above, the students were all studying seed dispersal. They were given the opportunity to do so in a way that interested and challenged them, and accommodated their particular abilities. They worked on a variety of tasks, many of them self-directed, using a range of materials. In other words, the seed-dispersal lesson was tiered.

Tiering should be done in a way that makes it invisible to students. Children can be told that they are working on different assignments or with different materials so that they can share what they've done with the class. Students have opportunities to think, talk about, and identify what they want to learn, as well as how they want to learn it. When students are allowed some input on how they want to learn something, challenging a task in many different ways and with different materials or technologies becomes the norm. In every case, the work should be equally interesting and fair in terms of students' individual expectations and engagement.

## Scaffolding Learning

While tiering is a strategy to differentiate instruction within a whole classroom and is planned by the teacher, *scaffolding* is a concept that can apply directly to the work that EAs do with individual students.

Russian psychologist Lev Vygotsky (1978) developed the concept of the zone of proximal development (ZPD), describing it as the difference between what a student can do without help and what they can accomplish with competent assistance. Scaffolding occurs within the ZPD as the teacher or EA provides successive levels of temporary support so that students can acquire skills that they couldn't reach without support. In order to scaffold effectively, then, you need to know the ZPD for the child or children with whom you are working, then make the necessary accommodations or modifications.

Examples of scaffolding might include:

- Demonstrating what is to be done
- Teaching a new concept with a series of mini-lessons
- Describing concepts in multiple ways
- Giving students a model showing what is expected
- Drawing on the prior knowledge of the students
- Giving students time to discuss new information
- Using visual aids
- Reviewing material in advance and preteaching vocabulary
- Giving students time to practice
- Stopping often to review and check for understanding

## Differentiating Instruction for Particular Exceptionalities

Never reduce a child to their exceptionality. Every child is unique—in temperament, in appearance, in interests, in life experience, in ability. However, the exceptionality that a child has, whether it is intellectual, behavioural, communicative, physical, linguistic, or a combination of these, does shape some aspects of their life. Considering the impact of the exceptionality on the child's life helps us to know how to support them in their learning. For this reason, we've included a chart in Appendix C that shows challenges and possible supports associated with particular exceptionalities.

It's very important to recognize that children will probably not fit neatly into the categories in this chart. They may, for instance, have several exceptionalities: a student with a learning disability may also have ADHD. Children with other exceptionalities may also be gifted, but their exceptionalities may make it difficult to recognize their giftedness. All children, regardless of exceptionalities, have strengths.

As an EA, you play an important role in assisting students to become successful learners. Knowing how academic skills develop helps you assess the child's skill level and support their further development. Similarly, understanding social development—the topic of Chapter 11—helps you know how to help children get along socially.

## Individualized Education Plan (IEP)

Students who have exceptionalities will usually have an *individualized education plan* (IEP). This may be required by the government, school district, or principal. A courtesy IEP may also be requested by the family. It is developed by the teacher with the involvement of the EA and parents or guardians. Different jurisdictions refer to this plan using different titles, including individualized learning plan (ILP), student learning plan (SLP), or individualized program plan (IPP). Other terminology may be used on documents for early learners (preschool and kindergarten). Although they have different names, the purpose of each of these plans is essentially the same: to develop a specialized plan to support the child's learning.

The process of developing an IEP begins with the identification of a student who is at risk of not succeeding in school. Different school jurisdictions use different screening procedures and assessment tools. The EA may have a role in collecting data and administering some informal assessments, though they will not be involved in interpreting that data.

If it is decided that a student requires an IEP, the teacher will typically draft one, then consult with the student's parents or guardians and the school administration. They will have input and sign off on the plan, and will meet to review the IEP during and at the end of the year. If the EA is available, they will sit in on these meetings.

The input from parents or guardians is vitally important because they bring a perspective that comes from living with the student outside of school and over a period of time. They can describe the child's strengths, the challenges they see, and their hopes and dreams for the child. They can comment on the child's overall school experience and what they think the teacher and school need to do to address their child's learning needs. Once the plan has been established, they may be able to reinforce some aspects with the student at home and can report on progress at the review meetings.

Appendices A and B help to illustrate this process. Appendix A is an Inclusive Community Planning Matrix. This matrix could be used as a method of planning for purposeful, meaningful, and relevant inclusion opportunities in various school settings. Appendix B is a sample IEP form.

## The EA's Role in Differentiating Instruction for IEPs

Planning to differentiate learning rests primarily with the teacher and is outlined in the IEP. The work of implementing the IEP, however, rests largely with the EA. Below is a checklist to guide you in this work. The list is meant to point to possible considerations in the implementation of an IEP. You may not check every box in every instance.

- Begin with the child's strengths, and build on their existing knowledge and skills.
- Adapt or modify the learning task so the child will address it at their own skill level. The concept of scaffolding, discussed above, is useful here.
- Be sure that you fully understand the skills being taught. For example, if you are teaching mathematics, you must understand the concept of number sense.
- Use assistive and adaptive technology to support learning.
- Understand the purpose of an assignment and adapt or modify the instruction to align with that goal.
- Vary instructional methods so that learning is accessible in many ways.
- Make the instructional method engaging and flexible so that everyone will be able to understand.
- Give specific feedback frequently. This gives the student the opportunity to recognize what they have learned.
- Use ongoing assessment of student progress and adapt your instruction as necessary.
- Model strategies to students who will not develop strategies on their own.
- Break an assignment into small, manageable tasks.

## Providing Tactful Support

At the beginning of this chapter you met Romy, who didn't want to admit that she didn't understand a task. Many students, like Romy, resent or are embarrassed that they require extra help with their school tasks. Sometimes it's easier for them to approach a classmate for help than to ask an EA or teacher, and they should be encouraged to do that. Never *assume* that a student needs help, but if it appears that they might, just ask them. If Nasima is staring at an assignment when her classmates are moving on with it, and you believe from past experience that she may need assistance, you can quietly ask, "Can I help you get started with this?" Be prepared to back away if she says no. When you do provide assistance, do so quietly and unobtrusively.

You will also encounter students who ask for help before they need it, possibly out of avoidance, lack of confidence, or difficulties processing oral directions. If you know them well, you will understand when help is truly needed. To support them in becoming independent learners, be sure you provide just enough assistance to help them get started. You might ask, "Can you remember doing a question like this before? How did you do it?" or, "What do you think might be the first thing to do?"

The goal of raising children who feel valued, capable, and have a sense of belonging can guide your interactions and decisions in your role as an EA. This will be particularly important and challenging if you are working with a child or children who have special needs that set them apart from the rest of a class. You can ask yourself:

- Is this setting/activity/interaction building this child's sense of worth, of competence, of belonging?
- How am I helping children set their own goals and build pride in their accomplishments regardless of what others are doing?
- How can I create activities that give this child a sense of belonging and contributing to the group?
- In what ways am I letting this child know that I appreciate them for who they are?
- What are this child's strengths, and how can I help them build on these strengths?

This chapter has introduced you to the concept of universal design for learning (UDL) and the theory that supports it. You've had an opportunity to see the kind of planning that might occur within a UDL classroom. The next chapters will expand on the idea of differentiated instruction by looking specifically at differentiating instruction for the development of academic and social skills.

## Takeaways

- Universal design for learning (UDL) uses curriculum design and technologies to make learning accessible to all students.
- UDL classrooms use differentiated instruction (DI) strategies, including tiering and scaffolding.
- EAs differentiate by accommodating and adapting instruction and modifying curriculum.
- Individual education plans (IEPs) guide instruction for students with exceptionalities.
- Technologies can assist students with exceptionalities to perform classroom tasks. Being familiar with these technologies is usually the responsibility of the EA.
- Technology is making it possible for increasing numbers of children with exceptionalities to reach high academic goals.
- Every child is unique, but children who have particular exceptionalities may benefit from certain adaptations, modifications, or accommodations.

## Reflection and Discussion

- The beginning of this chapter profiled several students with varying learning needs. Imagine that you are a student in their classroom. What are some of the ways that your individual learning needs might be met, and your strengths showcased? What might an IEP for you look like?

# 10

# Supporting Academic Learning: Inquiry, Literacy, and Numeracy

*The art of teaching is the art of assisting discovery.*

—*MARK VAN DOREN*

## Learning Outcomes

After reading this chapter, you will be able to answer these questions:

- What do we mean when we use the term *emergent* to describe literacy, numeracy, or inquiry skills?
- Why is it important to know how academic skills develop?
- Why is curiosity important to learning?
- What are some ways to support children's emergent literacy skills? Their emergent numeracy skills?

## Introduction

In Chapter 9, we considered some ways of differentiating instruction to meet the learning needs of all students. In this chapter, you will learn about how skills develop in the areas of inquiry, literacy, and numeracy. The chapter gives suggestions for ways that you, as an EA, can enhance student learning in each of these three important areas. It also includes resources for supporting academic skills for children with particular exceptionalities.

This chapter begins with inquiry skills because being curious is at the heart of learning. Children need to be encouraged to look at the world in a questioning way. Their curiosity is the basis for literacy and numeracy—the second and third topics in the chapter, respectively—because it leads them to look for answers and find ways to represent their learning.

You will find a huge range of development in each classroom. There may be children in your class who are reading fluently and others who are struggling to connect sounds with letters. Some may excel in math while others may have numeracy skills that are well below their grade level. As an EA, you will often be working with children whose skills are "emerging," or in early stages of development. Knowing how skills typically develop allows you to assess each child's development and helps you scaffold their learning to the next level.

Skills in literacy and numeracy vary within a classroom, and even vary from child to child. A child with advanced numeracy skills may struggle with reading. Each child is on a personal journey in developing their emergent skills. Like any other development process, mastery of emergent skills leads to later mastery of more complex skills. These skills are interrelated and may develop in parallel or overlap.

Some children arrive at school having developed many early skills. If their families have read to them from an early age, they might already understand a great deal about the potential of books and how they work. If their childcare centre has given them many opportunities to explore with objects, they may have built a good foundation for numeracy.

Unfortunately, not all children have the same opportunities to develop these crucial emergent skills. Many children face challenges; however, with early identification of learning difficulties, support for families, and appropriate interventions, they can be set on an optimal pathway to reach their full potential. Early intervention is critical because difficulties can persist and affect further learning throughout the school years.

## Supporting Inquiry: The Importance of Asking Questions

Remember the classroom we visited in Chapter 9? It was a grade 4 class where children were learning about seed dispersal, and were engaged in a variety of activities: researching and making notes for a movie, constructing a poster and 3-dimensional sculptures of seeds, gluing different kinds of seeds onto a poster, and working with an EA to find books about plants and seeds. This was a snapshot of a universal design learning (UDL) classroom: one that showed an environment where each child could work according to their own skills and participate at their own level.

Let's consider what might have happened before this snapshot of the classroom. How did the children become so involved in their investigations? Their teacher tells us that their interest grew from a discussion about whether carnivorous plants had seeds and, if they did, how they would spread them. They went on to brainstorm other questions about seeds and became excited about learning how different kinds of plants disperse their seeds. These are *inquiry skills* in action. Learning grows from questions, and their preliminary discussion about plants and seeds left these children with a desire to know that carried them through days of investigation.

Now let's consider some of the skills the children demonstrated in their activities. Certainly, these children were using their diverse literacy skills: the children who are competent readers were doing research, while a child who is an emergent reader was looking for books with an EA. They were working on representing their learning in various ways, including a movie and a sculpture. Early numeracy skills were also involved as children sorted and classified the various kinds of seeds.

This scenario illustrates an important concept: that literacy, numeracy, and inquiry skills are intertwined. Inquiry skills are about an attitude of curiosity and question-asking, while literacy skills make it possible to find and communicate answers to those questions. Numeracy skills supplement literacy skills by making it possible to organize and represent learnings in different and useful ways.

## Inquiry Skills

Children begin using inquiry skills from the moment they are born. As babies, they form ideas about the world around them. As they grow, they continue to use their own ideas to make sense of new events. With curiosity and imagination, children ask questions about their surroundings. *Why are the rabbits changing colour? How long is an earthworm? Why does ice turn to water?* They interact, explore, and inquire.

Children take an active role in developing their understanding of the world and how things work. They learn best through mental and physical activity: when they work things out on their own and interact with others rather than receiving and carrying out explicit instruction.

As an EA, it is your role to support children as they develop inquiry skills. You will scaffold skills (see "Scaffolding Learning," Chapter 9), finding that fine line between providing supportive comments and questions to guide and encourage students' exploration and simply telling them the answers. Resist the urge to answer students' questions for them; being *told* why ice turns to water, for example, is not nearly as meaningful or memorable for a student as finding out the answer for themselves.

Below is a list of inquiry skills, along with interventions and phrases an EA can use to help students develop them. These are skills children use throughout their lives to answer questions about the world. In school, children utilize inquiry skills in every subject. Science in particular draws upon inquiry skills.

**TABLE 10.1. Inquiry Skills and Effective EA Interventions**

| SKILL | TO SUPPORT LEARNING THROUGH INQUIRY THE EA WILL: | TO SUPPORT LEARNING THROUGH INQUIRY THE EA WILL SAY: |
|---|---|---|
| **Explore objects, materials, and events** | • Provide opportunities for investigating materials, objects, and phenomena firsthand, online, or in books | • How do you think this happened?'<br>• What do you notice about these objects that is the same / different? |
| **Make careful observations** | • Provide time and opportunity for observations | • Take the time to look carefully and think about what you are seeing. |
| **Use a variety of simple tools to gather information** | • Teach the correct use of tools that extend the senses (e.g., magnifying glasses) measure change (e.g., thermometers) or measure differences (e.g., rulers) | • How much (longer, heavier, etc.) is this than…?<br>• Were you expecting to see this? |
| **Record observations using words, pictures, charts, and graphs** | • Provide materials and tools to record their data<br>• Scaffold guidance as needed | • How are you going to keep a record of what you do and find?<br>• What kind of (chart, graph, drawing, etc.) do you think is the best way to show the results? |
| **Develop tentative explanations and ideas** | • Ask questions that require the use of these skills (and allow time for thinking about and answering those questions) | • Why do you think that happened?<br>• What will you need to do to find out…? |

| SKILL | TO SUPPORT LEARNING THROUGH INQUIRY THE EA WILL: | TO SUPPORT LEARNING THROUGH INQUIRY THE EA WILL SAY: |
|---|---|---|
| **Ask questions** | • Show interest in the children's answers to their questions | • What would you like to know about…? <br> • Is this what you were expecting? |
| **Describe characteristics (including shape, size, pattern, and number), compare, sort, classify, and order** | • Model descriptive vocabulary for size, shape, characteristics | • Did you find any similarity between… and …? <br> • What characteristic are you using for your system of sorting/ classifying? |
| **Work collaboratively with others** | • Encourage, through example, tolerance, mutual respect, and objectivity in discussions and learning tasks | • How can you explain to the others what you did and what happened? |
| **Share and discuss ideas and listen to new perspectives** | • Show interest when others are talking | • How can you show what you discovered? <br> • What interests you about what you are hearing? |

Students who have good literacy skills can find answers to the questions they ask and can effectively organize and convey the information that they gather. As we will see in the next section, learning to read, write, listen, and speak are complex processes that begin early in life.

# Supporting Literacy

> Eight-month-old Emily sits on her mother's knee while her brother Anthony, who is two-and-a-half, cuddles beside them in the comfy chair. They are reading a children's book in which every page ends with, "And then she saw…" Anthony knows the book well and he repeats the phrase loudly and enthusiastically just before they turn each page.

Emily and Anthony are well on their way to literacy. As you read through this section, you'll see why we call them *emergent readers*.

## What Is Literacy?

In the traditional sense, literacy is the ability to read, write, listen, and speak in order to communicate effectively and make sense of the world. Literacy development begins at birth and continues through adulthood. The early learning of literacy from birth to kindergarten is called *emergent literacy*. As the internet and emerging technologies advance and impact our lives, the definition of literacy is continually changing to reflect the needs of the twenty-first century learner (Leu, 2000).

## Emergent Literacy

Emergent literacy has to do with building foundational skills for later reading and writing. The components of emergent literacy are:

- Motivation to read
- Sound awareness
- Concepts of print
- Alphabet knowledge
- Oral language skills

We will look at what each of these means and how you, as an EA, can support children in developing these skills.

### Motivation to read

Being motivated to read involves the enjoyment of books and reading. Children who love hearing books and stories read aloud to them tend to be curious about reading and motivated to learn to read. This is important because learning to read is a gradual, ongoing process that needs motivation to succeed.

Here are some ways that you can encourage children's motivation to read:

- Make reading a special, shared, fun time.
- Read everywhere! Draw attention to environmental print wherever you see it: signs, logos, recipes…
- Follow the child's interests; allow them to choose the books they want to read.
- Enjoy books with predictable text or rhymes so children can read along with you.
- Read with expression. Use different voices for different characters, let your face and voice show what the characters are feeling.
- Set an example by showing your enjoyment of reading.
- Ensure the child can see your face and the book at the same time.
- Talk about the pictures and relate the pictures to the child's life.

- Point to some words while reading to show that the writing on a page has meaning.
- Alter activities when the child loses interest. Don't worry about finishing a book.
- Use interactive book reading. Have a conversation or activity to do with each page.
- Head to the library regularly.

### Sound awareness

The term *sound awareness* refers to the ability to distinguish and work with sounds. At the emergent literacy level this means being able to recognize rhymes, syllables, and segment, and to blend sounds together to form words. Sound awareness is foundational to being able to sound out words.

Here are some ways to encourage children to become aware of sounds:

- Read books with rhyming patterns and sing songs.
- Ask children to come up with words that rhyme or start with the same sound.
- Play with tongue twisters.
- Pick a sound for the day. Notice the sound at the beginning or end of words.
- Use apps and other technologies to learn and practice phonological or phonemic awareness skills.
- Use blocks to build words and take them apart.

### Concepts of print

Children who develop the concepts of print have a better understanding of how reading works (Holdgreve-Resendez, 2010). The broadest concept of print is *print awareness:* the understanding that print has meaning, that we are surrounded by print, and that print follows a set of rules.

Here are some ways to encourage print awareness:

- Use environmental print to point out letters, words, spaces, and lines of print.
- Read lots of picture books aloud and point out the concepts of print—for example, first or last word in a sentence, or certain letters in a story.
- Use nursery rhymes, room item labels, name cards, and so on to help children recognize words that are important to them.
- Use magnetic letters, alphabet-shaped cereal, and games to develop the concept of a letter.
- Display an alphabet chart or use an alphabet border strip to talk about letters.

- Practice recognizing upper- and lowercase letters using manipulatives.
- To develop the concept of a word, count the number of words in a line of print.
- Write out a sentence that a child has said onto two sentence strips. Cut one strip into the individual words in the sentence, and encourage the child to match these words to the complete strip. Point out the first word, last word, and other aspects of the sentence.
- Plan a scavenger hunt to find letters, words, sentences, punctuation, and uppercase letters in books.

*Book awareness* is another concept of print that includes understanding what a book is, how to hold a book, and how to turn pages.

These are some ways to encourage book awareness:

- Provide daily opportunities to participate in shared reading and paired reading.
- During paired reading, use an older student to read while the younger student follows along with their finger.
- Point out the parts of books, including the top and bottom of a page, where you begin reading, the first word, and so on.
- Model reading from left to right by running your finger under the print as you read.
- Have the student run their finger under the words as you read a story.
- Point out differences in various types of books (e.g., story books, poems, information books, etc.) and how they are organized.

### Alphabet knowledge

The term *alphabet knowledge* refers to knowing the individual letter names, sounds, and shapes. During the emergent literacy level, children learn to "crack" the alphabetic code—that is, the understanding that there is a correspondence between written letters and the sounds of the spoken language, and that this correspondence is predictable and systematic. The importance of alphabet knowledge to literacy cannot be understated. Many recognize it as the best predictor of later achievement in literacy (Jones, Clark, & Reutzel, 2013).

Here are some ways to support alphabet knowledge:

- Point out letters and print in the environment.
- Provide activities to play with letter shapes and sounds.
- Read alphabet books and student names on charts, desks, and so on.
- Talk about letters and their sounds when seen in everyday life.
- Play sound matching games and sorting activities.

- Sing the ABCs and recite rhymes.
- Play with letter shapes (magnets, blocks, dough letters, etc.).
- Introduce letter–sound correspondence using high-use letters and those with sounds that are distinctively different.

### Oral language skills

Oral language skills include ability to listen, share knowledge, describe things and events, and tell stories. They are considered to be the foundation for developing literacy skills (Bradfield et al., 2013). There are two types of oral language skills: listening (*receptive language*) and speaking (*expressive language*).

Narrative skills are also part of oral language skills and fall under the category of speaking skills. Narrative skills include the ability to tell stories, entertain, report and retell events, tell others about ourselves, and persuade.

These are some ways you can encourage the development of oral language skills:

- Initiate play and conversation whenever possible.
- Have daily one-on-one conversations.
- Talk to the child frequently using different and interesting words.
- Listen to stories and information at a listening centre.
- Preteach new vocabulary and regularly review previously taught vocabulary.
- Explicitly teach abstract words and their meanings.
- Model how to use language correctly.
- Help children describe outings and past events or tell stories.
- Ask questions that help children learn to provide explanations and sequence events.
- Bring in photos of childhood or family events that spark an interest in sharing.
- Play talking and memory games. Let children explain the rules of the games.
- Practice following multiple-step directions.
- Use repetition frequently and ask children to paraphrase information in their own words.

## Learning to Read

Reading is basically the process of making meaning from print. When we read, we decode letters, punctuation marks, and spaces, and convert them into words and sentences that are meaningful for us. Although the process of learning to read can vary from child to child, there are certain developmental stages of reading that most children go through.

**TABLE 10.2. Developmental Reading Stages**

| DEVELOPMENTAL READING STAGE | SKILLS |
|---|---|
| Awareness and exploration | • Learns to hold a book<br>• Learns to turn pages<br>• Points to pictures and says a word or sound |
| Emergent reader | • Talks about the story or message in a book<br>• Begins to understand the relationship between the words and the pictures<br>• Begins to retell a story from the pictures |
| Early reader | • Learns the relationship between the letters and the sounds they make<br>• Learns that letters work together to make words that can be spoken or read<br>• Is able to read some high-frequency words |
| Transitional reader | • Reads familiar texts with increasing fluency<br>• Has learned to decode unfamiliar words<br>• Has a growing sight word vocabulary |
| Fluent reader | • Reads to acquire information and explore new ideas and feelings<br>• Reads a wide range of material<br>• Reads independently |

# Components of Reading

Ireland's National Council for Curriculum Assessment (2012) identifies five essential components of reading:

1. Motivation
2. Word identification skills
3. Vocabulary
4. Comprehension
5. Fluency

Let's look at each of these components in more detail, along with ways for you to support development in each area.

## Motivation

Student motivation is an influential factor in successful reading (Takaloo & Ahmadi, 2017). As a child reads more and more, the better they become at reading and the more they enjoy it! As stated before, learning to read is a gradual, ongoing process that needs motivation to succeed. Keeping children engaged and interested in reading is very important for their development.

Below are some ways you can increase children's interest in reading:

- Set aside a regular read-aloud time.
- Make reading fun. Consider using finger puppets and other props. Do funny voices as you read together.
- Make sure reading materials are at the child's reading ability.
- Use buddy reading. Create partner groups among students in class or with students from another class.
- Visit the library regularly and request a booklist for particular readers and their interests.
- Allow children to select the book of their choice within their reading level.
- Bring in books that feature topics or themes of interest to the child.
- Create fun projects that connect to the theme of their reading book.
- Use high-interest, low-vocabulary books or graphic novels for older readers.
- Find a chapter book series or a favourite genre to spark reading interest.

### Word identification skills

The term *word identification skills* refers to the ability to read words accurately and automatically. These skills help students decode words: figure out, pronounce, and understand them.

To build strong skills, the child needs to be able to use several *decoding strategies* such as:

- *Phonics*. Phonics teaches the principles of letter–sound relations for sounding out words.
- *Word families*. Students learn group of letters with a common pattern: hat, fat, rat, bat, sat…
- *Word chunking*. Students look for familiar letter chunks (e.g., sm<u>all</u>, <u>back</u>pack, ch<u>arm</u>).
- *Sight words*. These are words that don't follow rules of spelling and pronunciation (e.g., come, does, shoe).
- *High frequency words*. Students practice reading common words that they know well.
- *Context cues*. Students "read over" a word they don't know, look for context in the surrounding text, and come back to the unknown word later.
- *Picture cues*. Students look to pictures for support.

Some of the techniques EAs may consider when supporting children in building word identification include:

- Teaching phonics in a systematic, explicit way, moving from simple to complex
- Using computer programs for phonological skills
- Using predictable books, songs, poems, chants, and games
- Exploring letter–sound relationships using manipulatives (e.g., magnetic letters)
- Building word banks (e.g., index boxes) of sight words and new words as they are introduced
- Reinforcing the use of picture clues by practicing with picture books
- Practicing sounding out words (e.g., starting with the first letter in a word, say each letter sound aloud, then blend the sounds together and try to say the word)
- Practicing word chunking by looking for familiar letter chunks
- Reinforcing prefixes, suffixes, endings, whole words, and base words
- Encouraging students to connect to a word they know in order to decode an unfamiliar word

## *Vocabulary*

A child's vocabulary is their knowledge of words and their meanings. It plays an important role in the reading process and in the child's ability to comprehend a story.

A reader cannot understand a text without knowing most of the words. Most children learn words naturally through everyday experiences; however, some words need to be intentionally taught. There are differences between our listening, speaking, reading and writing vocabularies.

Some ways to help children build their vocabulary are:

- Using videos and visuals to expand word meaning
- Building word banks (e.g., index box) of key vocabulary to review frequently
- Explicitly discussing the meanings of new words
- Reinforcing strategies for deciphering unknown words such as understanding prefixes, suffixes, and roots
- Using many vocabulary games and introducing weekly challenge words
- Preteaching new vocabulary and concepts prior to reading a book
- Teaching students when and how to use a dictionary, thesaurus, and other reference aids

- Choosing reading materials that help the student become familiar with increasingly high levels of words
- Teaching and extending vocabulary and conceptual knowledge through concept words, positional words, calendar concepts, and time-related words
- Repeating vocabulary words across different activities and subjects

### Comprehension

Reading comprehension is the ability to read written words and understand the overall meaning or idea. It is also the ability to make connections between what children know and what they have read.

Some ways to help children build their comprehension are:

- Helping students learn to use pictures in books to help them understand the contents
- Encouraging children to read aloud
- Using a ruler or finger to encourage students to follow along the line of print
- Reading books in short sections and making sure students know what happened in the story (building paraphrasing skills) before continuing on
- Encouraging children to write down unfamiliar words and look them up later
- Having children generate questions prior to reading a book
- Helping students learn to skim the headings in a text to give them an overall view of what the text is about
- Encouraging students to reread challenging areas of a text that they don't understand
- Talking about what children have read or learned after reading
- Encouraging the retelling of a story using a logical sequence
- Using graphic organizers to help students keep track of what they have read or heard
- Having students recap and summarize main points after reading to ensure they understand what has been read
- Reinforcing effective comprehension strategies one skill at a time

### Fluency

Fluency is the ability to read with speed, accuracy, and proper expression. Fluent readers are able to read in phrases with proper intonation. Their reading is smooth and expressive.

Here are some ways to support children in becoming more fluent readers:

- Read aloud to children to provide an example of fluent reading.

- Have children follow along with stories at a listening centre.
- Read nursery rhymes, songs, and funny poems for choral reading. Choral reading is everyone reading together at the same time.
- Practice sight words for rapid recall and smoother reading. Use fun activities (e.g., bingo games, flashcards, slapping sight word cards that are called out, etc.).
- Have the student do a lot of reading at an independent reading level. Read books over and over again for speed, accuracy, and expression.
- Use paired reading, placing a fluent reader with a less fluent reader for practice.
- Read poetry.
- Read a reader's theatre piece.

## Instructional Strategies and Methods for Reading

While working in schools, you will be exposed to many educational terms and names of methods, strategies, and techniques for teaching literacy. You may be expected to guide a small group of learners or support a specific child using a particular method. Being aware of these terms and what they mean will help you provide the most effective assistance.

### Guided reading

In *guided reading*, a small group of students who are grouped according to reading ability read with a teacher or EA. The educator introduces the book and vocabulary and sets a purpose for reading. They guide the children as they read, reinforcing reading strategies and encouraging students to make predictions. After reading, the student's comprehension skills are strengthened through questioning, discussion, and follow-up activities. The teacher or EA provides direction and scaffolding to develop reading strategies. An essential component of guided reading is the use of *levelled reading books*: reading material that has been coded with a specific level of readability (Fountas & Pinnell, 1996).

### Independent reading

In independent reading, students read a text independently and often choose the book themselves. A book that is considered to be at a child's *independent reading level* is a book the child can comfortably read and comprehend without the support of an adult.

### Partner reading

In *partner reading*, two students collaborate to read or reread a book together to practice fluency. Children can take turns reading by sentence, paragraph, or page.

### Shared reading

*Shared reading* is when a teacher or EA reads aloud while students follow along using copies of the same book, a big book, or a book on the interactive white board. The teacher models fluent reading and gives opportunities for the students to echo-read or work on developing their reading strategies (Tompkins, Bright & Winsor, 2018).

### Readers' workshops

*Readers' workshops* encourage students to use three stages of reading: pre-reading, reading, and response. First, students choose books, set purposes, and make plans as they begin to read. Next, they read the book independently. After reading, they complete an activity such as writing in a reading log, discussing their book, or completing a book project. (Tompkins, Bright & Winsor, 2018)

### Literature circles

A *literature circle* is a book club that is geared specifically to developing literacy. Students meet in small groups to discuss a book that the group has chosen. Each member of the circle is assigned a specific role that helps guide the discussion (Tompkins, Bright & Winsor, 2018).

### Think–pair–share

*Think–pair–share* is a collaborative learning strategy in which students work together to solve a problem or answer a question about an assigned reading or question. This method maximizes student participation as children are more comfortable presenting ideas to the group with the support of a partner. Students think through questions using three steps (Solomon, 2009):

1. *Think.* Students think individually about a topic or answer to a question.

2. *Pair.* Students share ideas and thoughts with their partner.

3. *Share.* Student pairs share their ideas with the larger group or class.

## Supporting Writing

> Ash's father is writing a grocery list and three-year-old Ash wants to help. She brings a pencil and paper, sits beside him, and fills her paper with wavy lines.

Writing is one of the most challenging tasks for children to learn. This is because a number of skills are involved in expressing thoughts in writing. The art of writing takes time and practice to learn, and the learning of these skills is neither linear nor sequential. Knowledge, focus, memory, visual and fine motor skills, and patience play big roles in writing and learning to write. Keep in mind that each child is on their own personal learning journey as they develop these skills.

## Visual and Fine Motor Skills for Writing

A child needs these visual and fine motor skills in order to print by hand:
- Small muscle control
- Hand-eye coordination
- Ability to hold a writing tool
- Ability to smoothly form strokes and shapes
- Ability to visually perceive likeness and differences
- Ability to place and control the paper

For some children who struggle with visual and fine motor skills, writing is a very challenging skill to develop. Assistive technology could be considered as a means of support for these children.

## Cognitive Skills for Writing

Children also need certain cognitive skills to support their writing, including:
- Sounding out words
- Having a good vocabulary
- Understanding textual organization
- Knowing what to write about
- Producing words in print by printing by hand or typing; spelling; and/or using assistive technologies such as speech-to-text, word prediction, spelling and grammar check, digital thesauruses
- Being able to write sentences that make sense
- Being able to plan what to write, draft, revise, and edit
- Knowing that there are different types or genres of writing (e.g., story writing, poetry writing, etc.)
- Being able to self-regulate while in the writing process and use self-talk

## Writing Stages

Children begin writing long before entering kindergarten. As shown in the chart below, writing skills tend to progress through common stages, though not necessarily in sequential order. Always promote a positive attitude towards writing, both yours and the students'. Provide supportive comments as shown in the "Ways to support development" column.

**TABLE 10.3. The Stages of Writing Development and How EAs Can Support Them**

| WRITING STAGE | CHARACTERISTICS OF WRITING STAGE | WAYS EAs CAN SUPPORT DEVELOPMENT |
|---|---|---|
| **Drawing** | • Large, random, circular lines<br>• Writer believes images represent writing and convey a message | • Model writing in a variety of contexts<br>• Read a variety of books to writer<br>• Ask, "What are you writing about?" |
| **Scribbling** | • Smaller, curvy lines and shapes<br>• Writer uses scribbles to represent writing<br>• Scribbles are intentional<br>• Writer begins to hold writing tools as they have seen modeled | • Label items<br>• Read a variety of books to writer<br>• Ask, "What are you writing about?", "Would you like to write about...?" |
| **Mark writing** | • Zig-zagging lines<br>• Straight lines that run across the page | • Read a variety of books to writer<br>• Model writing in a variety of contexts<br>• Ask, "Would you tell me about what you are writing?" |
| **Mock letters** | • Forms resemble letters or common words from environmental print<br>• May be combined with mark making<br>• No intentional spaces between letters | • Read a variety of books to writer<br>• Write stories together with writer, repeating words after they are written<br>• Say, "You are working hard on your writing."<br>• Ask, "Would you like to tell me about your writing?" |
| **Letter strings** | • Writer moves from mock letters to real letters<br>• Writer starts to put letters together in a string | • Write books together (fiction and nonfiction)<br>• Write stories together, repeating words after they are written |

(continued on next page)

**TABLE 10.3. Continued**

| WRITING STAGE | CHARACTERISTICS OF WRITING STAGE | WAYS EAs CAN SUPPORT DEVELOPMENT |
|---|---|---|
| | • Upper- and lowercase letters may be mixed<br>• Letters may be of different sizes<br>• No spaces<br>• Writer begins to write their own name<br>• Writer begins to read their own writing<br>• Writer begins to understand a one-to-one correlation between written and spoken words<br>• Writer understands that print carries messages | • Ask, "What are you writing about?", "Can you tell me the story you are writing?" Don't expect the story to be the same every time they tell it to you |
| Transitional writing<br><br>EXIT ʊ Z<br>CT Rb | • Some spaces between letters<br>• Writer can copy environmental print<br>• Upper- and lowercase letters may be mixed<br>• Writer shows understanding that words are made from different letters<br>• Writer begins to see the difference between a letter and a word | • Provide functional writing opportunities (e.g., lists, notes, cards)<br>• Write stories together<br>• Ask, "Would you read me what you have written?" |
| Simple words and phrases<br><br>l LKb<br>Cts | • Inconsistent use of spaces<br>• Upper- and lowercase letters are mixed<br>• Writer can sound out some letters | • Provide functional writing opportunities (e.g., lists, notes, observations)<br>• Write stories together<br>• Provide opportunities for writer to share their work with others<br>• Ask, "Would you read me what you have written?" |

| WRITING STAGE | CHARACTERISTICS OF WRITING STAGE | WAYS EAs CAN SUPPORT DEVELOPMENT |
|---|---|---|
| **Initial and final consonants**<br><br>*Mi Dg is by* (handwritten) | • Spaces between words<br>• Writer may compose more than one sentence<br>• Writer shows increased understanding of letter sounds and spelling patterns and can use them in writing<br>• Writer may spell high-frequency words appropriately | • Provide functional writing exercises (e.g., lists, notes, cards, observations, journal)<br>• Write stories together<br>• Provide opportunities for writer to share their work with others<br>• Ask, "Would you read me what you have written?" |
| **Adding vowels**<br><br>*Leus r folNg* (handwritten) | • Writer attempts to add vowel sounds<br>• Writer may mix upper- and lowercase letters<br>• Ideas are present in writing | • Provide functional writing exercises (e.g., lists, letters, notes, messages observations, journal)<br>• Provide opportunities for writer to share their work with others<br>• Write stories together<br>• Ask, "Would you please read to me what you have written?" |
| **Sight words**<br><br>*THe old dog is blk.* (handwritten) | • Words are readable<br>• Writer is increasingly able to recall the spelling of high-frequency words<br>• Writer develops a personal style of writing<br>• Writer is learning to control conventions (e.g., spelling, punctuation, uppercase letters)<br>• Vocabulary expands (they begin writing more words than they use in their speech.)<br>• Writing is clear and understandable | • Provide functional writing (e.g., lists, letters, messages, schedules, calendars)<br>• Write stories together<br>• Ask, "Would you read what you have written to me please?"<br>• Provide opportunities for writer to share their work with others |

*(continued on next page)*

**TABLE 10.3. Continued**

| WRITING STAGE | CHARACTERISTICS OF WRITING STAGE | WAYS EAs CAN SUPPORT DEVELOPMENT |
|---|---|---|
| Purposeful writing | • Writer can tell a story or retell an event in writing<br>• Writer can record an event or information in writing<br>• Writer can make a list<br>• Writer can write emails, text messages, and letters<br>• Writer can write a reading response | • Provide meaningful opportunities for writing<br>• Expose writer to a wide range of writing<br>• Give opportunities to respond to the writing of others.<br>• Ask, "Who are you writing to?", "What is the purpose of your writing?" |
| Genres of writing | • Writer can write in a variety of genres, perhaps including:<br> › Persuasive<br> › Narrative<br> › Article<br> › Poetry<br> › Essay<br> › Fantasy<br> › Horror<br> › Romance<br> › Descriptive<br> › Expository<br> › Journals and letters | • Ask, "What are some of the words we use with a certain type of writing?", "How do we organize…?", "What is the goal of your writing?" |

# Building Writing Skills

Some ways to help children build their writing skills are:

- Helping students practice printing with letters of a consistent size that stay between the lines
- Using interlined pages or darkened lines to help students position letters
- Using a clean popsicle stick (hint: try putting a fun face on it and giving it a name!) or just a fingertip as a tool for creating spaces between words
- Using speech-to-text technology or scribing for children who struggle with the fine motor skill of printing

- Talking about personal experiences to stimulate ideas, then writing about them
- Helping students learn how to build better sentences by using adjectives and adverbs
- Working on how to split and combine sentences using connector words / conjunctions (i.e., and, or, but, etc.)
- Using the "hamburger" strategy to help students plan a paragraph: topic sentence (top bun), main idea and supporting details (patty), and conclusion (bottom bun)
- Brainstorming lots of ideas before writing
- Targeting writing to improve only one skill at a time so students will not become frustrated
- Comparing examples of different types of writing and how they are organized

## Supporting Numeracy

Two-year-old Ivy has gathered pinecones from around the yard and is arranging them in a line on the deck. As she does so she "counts": 1, 2, 3, 8, 4... Her five-year-old brother, Liam, is collecting stones and separating them into piles according to their shape and colour.

Numeracy, like literacy, is a skill that we need in order to fully participate in society. This section outlines the stages of numeracy development that form the basis for more complex mathematical operations down the road.

### What Is Numeracy?

As early learners develop their emergent literacy skills, they also begin to develop their understanding of numeracy. *Numeracy* is the ability to use numbers and spatial information to solve problems in real life. Numeracy skills begin to develop in infancy and the preschool years as children explore with concrete objects.

Before they reach school age or in the early years of formal education, many of a child's foundational math skills have been developed. When they enter school—and, therefore, formal math instruction—the curriculum builds each year on these same emergent skills, spiraling them to a deeper and deeper understanding and application of these principles.

In Canada, each provincial or territorial government has approved their own math curriculum. There are, however, five strands or areas of focus that are common across the country.

## Common Mathematic Curricular Strands Across Canada

- *Numbers and number sense*: recognizing, counting, and organizing numbers
- *Patterns and algebra*: recognizing and manipulating patterns and symbols
- *Measurement*: measuring using nonstandard and standard units
- *Geometry and spatial skills:* recognizing and classifying 2- and 3-dimensional shapes
- *Statistics and probability*: analyzing patterns and making predictions based on those analyses

As a student progresses through the grades, the concepts in each of these strands take them into a deeper understanding of mathematics. As an EA, you may be asked to support a child in math, frequently in the area of number sense.

Number sense is important because it promotes confidence with numbers. Students learn that numbers are predictable and sensible. Students who do not have a strong understanding of number sense lack the basis for simple math, let alone more complex operations. Those who fail to develop this foundational knowledge will lag behind their classmates more and more as they progress through the grades.

### Emergent Numeracy Skills

Exploring numbers, visualizing numbers in many contexts, and relating numbers in different ways are components of emergent numeracy skills. The chart below lists emergent number sense skills and their characteristics. The last column also provides suggestions for supporting the learning of each skill.

The progress that students make as they develop their literacy and numeracy skills is not completely predictable, but knowing how these skills tend to develop will help you identify their skill level and know what you can do to scaffold their learning. This knowledge is especially important for you as an EA because you will often be working with children whose level of skill is far different from their grade level. Many of these children have particular exceptionalities that you can take into account when working with them and planning learning strategies.

TABLE 10.4. Emergent Number Sense Skills and How EAs Can Support Them

| EMERGENT NUMBER SENSE SKILL | CHARACTERISTICS OF SKILL | WAYS EAs CAN SUPPORT LEARNING |
|---|---|---|
| **Verbal counting** *1, 2, 4, 9* | • Counting numbers orally, not necessarily sequentially<br>• Inability to count collections of up to 10 objects<br>• Lacking knowledge of all the number words | • Sing number songs<br>• Model counting objects while pointing to them |
| **Object counting** *1 2 3 4 5* | • One-to-one correspondence of numbers and objects; each object has one assigned number<br>• Counting by 1s and always beginning at 1 when they count<br>• Ability to name the numerals 0–10 | • Practice identifying numerals<br>• Use words and symbols to identify how many objects there are<br>• Practice making groups of an identified number of objects<br>• Practice counting forwards and backwards in sequence<br>• Practice counting up to twenty objects |
| **Cardinality** *5!!!* | • Ability to understand that the last number counted is the total number of objects | • Practice adding two groups of objects<br>• Use "counting-on" strategy to solve addition problems<br>• Use "counting back" strategy to solve subtraction problems<br>• Have student form equal groups and find their total<br>• Practice counting to 100 |
| **Subitizing** | • Ability to instantly see and say how many objects there are (usually up to six objects, though more when using a grid or other organizational system) | • Practice using a grid or patterns to subitize numbers<br>• Use grids for addition and subtraction<br>• Compare numbers on a grid or in a pattern to show relations "equal to," "less than," and "greater than" |

*(continued on next page)*

TABLE 10.4. Continued

| EMERGENT NUMBER SENSE SKILL | CHARACTERISTICS OF SKILL | WAYS EAs CAN SUPPORT LEARNING |
|---|---|---|
| **Comparing** | • Ability to recognize the relations "greater than," "less than," and "equal to," as well as "longer than," and "shorter than" <br><br> • Ability to regroup and subitize numbers to determine a sum or difference | • Encourage use of forward and backward number sequences to solve addition and subtraction problems <br><br> • Encourage use of various strategies to determine relations "greater than," "less than," and "equal to," "longer than," and "shorter than" <br><br> • Encourage application of various strategies when solving operation tasks |
| **Operations** $+ - \times \div$ | • Ability to work with groups of objects to add, subtract, multiply, and divide | • Encourage use of manipulatives and knowledge of number patterns to perform calculations <br><br> • Encourage use of various calculation strategies to determine sum, difference, product, and quotient |

## Takeaways

- Learning begins with curiosity. We need to encourage children to look at the world in a questioning way.
- Literacy and numeracy skills develop in somewhat predictable stages, although the actual path of development may vary with individual children. Knowing the general patterns of skill development helps you to identify a child's progress and work to scaffold the child to the next level.
- Many of the children you will be working with may be at the early or "emergent" stages of skill development.
- There are many ways that you, as an EA, can help children become inquirers and support their development in literacy and numeracy.

 ## Reflection and Discussion

- Think back: How did you learn to read, to write, to do math, and when did that learning begin? Now that you understand the skills that build the foundations for learning in these areas, how do you think of your own learning journey and its timeline?

# Supporting Social Skills

*When everyone is included, everyone wins.*

—*JESSE JACKSON*

## Learning Outcomes

After reading this chapter, you will be able to answer these questions:

- Why are friendships important?
- How do we learn social skills?
- What are some things that can influence our ability to get along in social situations?
- How can we help children develop their social skills?
- What are ways to prevent and respond to bullying?

## Introduction

Think of the role that your friendships play in your life. Friends can give you self-confidence and a sense of belonging. They celebrate your successes with you and support you during difficult times. They boost your happiness and reduce your stress. Thinking about the benefits you derive from your friendships makes it easy to see that school can be an unhappy and lonely place for children who, like Delaney in the story below, are socially isolated.

> Last week when Erica, an EA, met with her mentor teacher, Irina, Irina mentioned that Delaney's mother had come to see her and was quite distressed because Delaney wasn't wanting to come to school. It was the first year that this had been a problem. Delaney seemed to enjoy grades 1 and 2, but this

year she has complained of stomach aches many mornings. A trip to the family physician found no physical cause and Delaney seems to be doing well academically. Irina asked Erica if she would spend some extra time observing Delaney to see if she could determine the problem.

Today, Erica discusses her observations with Irina. She has done a number of anecdotal observations and jotted down a few additional notes. She has also prepared a sociogram charting Delaney's interactions with her classmates. Erica explains to Irina that she has noticed that in the playground Delaney is either alone on a bench or standing with one of the playground supervisors. A telling observation in the classroom sees another child, Bethany, saying to a friend, "Let's not play with Delaney. She's weird." When the children choose partners for group work, Delaney stands back and waits for another child to approach her.

It becomes apparent that Delaney's reluctance to go to school might have to do with her social exclusion. Irina and Erica discuss what they can do to make her a part of the classroom group.

We spend a great deal of our time in social situations, and the quality of the interactions in these situations is important to our sense of wellbeing. Unfortunately, many children struggle with social skills, and this can be particularly true for students who have exceptionalities. It is unsurprising, then, that these individuals can be at greater risk for delinquency, depression, anxiety, and overall poorer postschooling outcomes (Walker & Barry, 2018)

In this chapter we will discuss factors that influence our development of social skills, the skills that children need to develop in order to get along with others, and how we can help them learn those skills. We also consider ways to detect when a child is being bullied and how to respond to bullying.

## The Development of Social Skills

Social skills can be described as the skills we need to interact with others in a way that is acceptable and appropriate. We begin to learn social skills as infants, when we cry to get our needs met, make eye contact, and smile at others. As preschoolers, we begin to learn to share toys and use words to communicate our wants and feelings.

Once we begin elementary school, we have many opportunities to form peer relationships, both in school and in extracurricular activities. It's then that we begin to have "best friends" and to develop more sensitivity to the feelings of others. As we proceed through upper elementary school, middle school, and high school, our family's influence on us decreases and peer interactions become more and more important.

## Factors Influencing Social Skills

Our social skills, like our neural functions, develop through a combination of genes and environment.

We are born with certain innate behaviour styles that comprise our temperament. Researchers have identified these styles in various ways. Chess and Thomas (1996), for example, describe nine characteristics of temperament:

1. *Activity*: how active the child is generally

2. *Distractibility*: degree to which a child can concentrate and pay attention when they are not especially interested

3. *Intensity*: how loud the child is

4. *Regularity*: the predictability of biological functions like appetite and sleep

5. *Sensory threshold*: how sensitive the child is to physical stimuli (e.g., touch, taste, smell, sound, light)

6. *Approach/Withdrawal*: characteristic responses a child has to new situations and strangers

7. *Adaptability*: how easily the child adapts to transitions and changes such as switching to a new activity

8. *Persistence*: how stubborn or unable to give up a child is

9. *Mood*: a child's tendency to react to the world primarily in a positive or negative way

These innate characteristics of temperament are then influenced as we grow by our environment and our experiences in the world, including our social experiences. At the same time, our temperament influences the kinds of experiences we have. For example, a child who is uncomfortable around strangers is unlikely to have the same social experiences as a child who is comfortable meeting new people.

Certain other characteristics, including appearance and what are sometimes called *molecular social skills*, influence our social acceptance. Molecular social skills include eye contact; rhythm, duration and content of speech; use of hand motions; and avoidance of unusual or annoying mannerisms (Kern, George & Weist, 2016). These are skills that can usually be taught.

Good social skills are highly dependent on effective communication abilities. Children with memory problems or with language and communication difficulties may be particularly vulnerable in social situations. They may have trouble keeping up with conversations or expressing their ideas to others. Other children may have difficulty reading nonverbal cues. Children with communication difficulties may act out their frustration with temper tantrums or other inappropriate behaviours, which further distances them from their peers. Helping them improve their communication skills will improve their social experience and their level of peer acceptance.

## What Social Skills Are Important?

Some of the social skills that are important for children to learn are:

- Greetings (including making eye contact)
- Initiating conversation (including finding topics that will interest and involve the other person)
- Turn-taking and reciprocity in conversations and in play
- Adapting what you are saying to the listener
- Taking the perspective of the other
- Empathizing
- Reading social cues
- Anticipating the response of the other before speaking
- Apologizing
- Problem-solving

# Strategies for Providing Social Supports

Children may be embarrassed by their lack of acceptance and be sensitive to interference in their social relationships. Research has also shown that children have fewer interactions with peers when an EA is close by. EAs and teachers should find ways to support social inclusion that are as unobtrusive and inconspicuous as possible. Causton-Theoharis (2009) recommends not sitting next to a student or removing a student from the classroom. Promote independence by gradually and systematically fading out cues.

Below are some strategies EAs can use to unobtrusively provide social support:

- Be alert to children who are being rejected, ignored, or bullied.
- Help children invite each other to socialize.
- Pair a socially disadvantaged child with a socially adept child.

- Encourage peer support.
- Involve children in collaborative rather than competitive learning activities.
- Identify and acknowledge the strengths of all children.
- Help other students to understand any accommodations or specific behaviours (but be aware of confidentiality).
- Create a positive learning environment in which diversity is valued and celebrated.
- Use social stories or real situations as a basis for role playing or problem solving. Don't single out a single child or a single group of children (i.e., children with exceptionalities); involve the whole class or a small, diverse group.

## Differentiating Social Instruction for Particular Exceptionalities

As we know, all children are different, so it's not appropriate to generalize about them based on their exceptionalities. However, sometimes their exceptionalities impose limits on what they can do or cause them to behave in ways that make it more difficult for them to make friends. Appendix D shows ways to support social skills for children with various exceptionalities.

# Preventing and Responding to Bullying

While you are on playground duty, you notice that a group of children are moving in an aggressive manner toward Angus, a boy who is new to school. As you watch, they shove him against a fence several times and gesture menacingly. When you approach, they walk away.

---

Alyssa seems increasingly isolated at school. You learn that some of her classmates have been circulating nasty posts about her online and that she has seen them.

---

A group of kindergarten children are calling one of their classmates "smelly."

Society is becoming aware of the devastating and lasting effects that bullying can have on children's emotional and physical wellbeing. Many schools have a zero-tolerance policy regarding bullying and actively work to help children recognize and respond to bullying. Still, instances of bullying, and particularly cyberbullying, persist. It will be important for you, as an EA, to familiarize yourself with your school's policies and practices around bullying and to ensure you know how to detect and respond to instances of bullying.

## The Causes of Bullying

Bullying can have a number of causes. Most are linked in some way to low self-esteem and/or jealousy on the part of the bully. Students who bully may be:

- Jealous of peers who seem accomplished and happy
- Reenacting harsh behaviour they have experienced at the hands of a family member
- Responding to judgmental views they have heard at home
- Trying to buy favour with a group of peers whom they see as desirable or powerful

## The Effects of Bullying

Bullying affects not only the person being bullied, but also the person who bullies and those who witness bullying. When bullying exists in a school, it has a toxic effect on the school environment. Being bullied has been linked to poor mental health, substance abuse, and suicide. Individuals who show bullying behaviour as children may continue to engage in risky and violent behaviour as adults. Even bystanders to bullying show negative effects such as increased mental health problems, substance abuse, and school absences.

## Signs of Bullying

Students are often reluctant to admit they are being bullied, so it's important to be alert to signs such as:

- Personality changes (e.g., increased anxiety, depression, anger, tearfulness)
- Self-deprecating remarks, which may reflect the slights of others
- Falling grades
- Negative attitudes about school or frequent absences
- Reluctance to go outside at recess
- Frequent health complaints

- Physical marks such as bruises or redness on skin
- Loss or destruction of property such as dirt or food on clothing or torn clothing
- Attempts to cover up a physical feature or other characteristic that others have ridiculed

## Suspected Bullying

If you think you spot signs of bullying, be extra vigilant. Observe interactions in the classroom and in the schoolyard. Bullying is most likely to happen in locations where students are relatively unsupervised, such as on the school bus, in the washrooms, changing for gym, during recess, or during the walk to school.

You can open up conversations with a child by asking questions about their experiences in these situations. Begin with general questions and move sensitively into questions about bullying behaviours.

Students might find it easier to tell you they have witnessed bullying than to admit that they have been bullied.

If you suspect bullying has been happening at recess, you might begin with these kinds of questions:

- Who did you play with at recess?
- Do you always play with…or do you sometimes play with someone else?
- Do you meet other kids when you're playing?

Then you can move to questions about behaviours:

- Do you ever see kids getting picked on or called names?
- Do you ever see kids taking someone else's toys?
- Do any of these things ever happen to you?
- Do you ever do any of these things to someone else?

You can also get a sense for how comfortable the student is with reporting the behaviour by asking:

- Have you talked with anyone at school about this?
- Do you think anyone who has seen this happening has reported it?

Be compassionate, calm, and nonjudgmental during these conversations so the student will feel safe talking with you about their experience.

## When a Student Discloses Bullying

If a student does disclose that they are being bullied, recognize the enormous trust they are placing in you by telling you about a delicate and personal situation. They are counting on you to respond appropriately and you want them to feel safe and supported.

Below is a checklist to help you navigate a disclosure of bullying:

- React calmly. Tell the student you are glad they shared the information with you. You could say, "It takes courage to speak up about something like this."
- Acknowledge the student's feelings. Don't tell them they are overreacting or that they shouldn't let it bother them. You might say, "I'm so sorry this is happening to you," or "What would you like me to do to help?"
- Realize that you might not have all of the relevant information, but don't pry.
- Give the student space to explain the problem; don't jump in with solutions. You could ask some questions to get specific information such as, "Has this person hurt you physically?" or "What are you afraid this person might do to you?"
- Don't imply that the student is at fault. *Why did you let them do that to you?* or *Why don't you stand up for yourself?* are statements that blame the victim. You might instead ask something like, "Why do you suppose they're doing this?"
- You could suggest some strategies such as walking away, telling an adult, or spending free time with peers who are safe.
- Tell the student that you have to tell the teacher and principal.
- Document the discussion and any observations you make.
- Ensure that the teacher and the principal are informed and that measures are taken to keep the child safe.
- Continue to support the child. You could say, "Remember that I told you that I would have to let Ms. G. and Ms. B. know? How are you feeling right now?"

As we have seen, social-emotional and academic wellbeing are closely intertwined. If a child is socially isolated, it is likely that their academic performance will suffer as well. EAs can help students learn skills that will help them form friendships and be accepted by their peers.

Children flourish in a positive environment, and one way to create that environment is to use positive strategies for guiding students' behaviour. Our next chapter describes approaches that you can use to prevent and respond to children's challenging behaviours.

## Takeaways

- Friends play a very important role in our lives.
- Some children may need help to develop skills for making and maintaining friendships. This might be particularly true for children who have exceptionalities.
- Bullying can be very harmful for the students being bullied, the bully, and the onlookers. It's important to know how to detect and respond to bullying.

 ## Reflection and Discussion

- It may be challenging for us to empathize with the bully and to begin to understand the depth and source of their feelings. Given what you know about what might be going on for the bully in their life, can you identify ways that you could help them find more positive ways to deal with their feelings?

**12**

# Positive Guidance Strategies

*Every day in a hundred small ways our children ask,*
*"Do you hear me?"*
*"Do you see me?"*
*"Do I matter?"*
*Their behavior often reflects our response.*

—*L.R. KNOST*

## Learning Outcomes

After reading this chapter, you will be able to answer these questions:

- What are some of the things that children might be communicating through their challenging behaviour?
- Why is self-awareness an important quality for an EA?
- How might trauma or toxic stress affect a child's behaviour?
- What are the goals of child guidance?
- Why is it important to approach a challenging behaviour in the least directive way possible?
- What is a continuum of guidance responses?

## Introduction

As an EA, you will work with many students who have behaviours that are challenging. This chapter will show you how to respond to difficult behaviours in ways that help maintain a positive classroom environment, let students feel respected, and support students in developing skills for *self-regulation*: the ability to exercise self-control over one's emotions and behaviours.

Annie, an EA, sees the last child onto the bus, waves, then slumps onto a nearby bench, the events of the day still occupying her mind: Sabrina's meltdown when she was faced with yet another math problem, Ahmed's lack of progress with reading and, most upsetting of all, Stephen swearing and spitting at her when she tried to get him to leave the gym. Until now, she'd thought they had a pretty good relationship.

Her mentor teacher, Bashir, notices her distress: "It was a rough day, wasn't it?"

"It was a terrible day," Annie moans. "I'm not sure I can do this."

Bashir, quietly sympathetic, urges her into the staff room and fixes her a cup of tea. After a few companionable minutes, Bashir asks, "Can you tell me a little more about Stephen? I haven't really had a chance to get to know him."

"I've met his mom," Annie replies. "She came in to tell me that Stephen will be away from school for a few days. His father has left them and she needs Stephen's help to look after his younger sister while she looks for a different apartment. I don't think she's working right now, so I'm guessing that they don't have a lot of money. She looked really overwhelmed."

"Poor Stephen. So many things at once—his dad leaving, moving to a new place, and possibly not a lot of money to spare," says Bashir.

"Yes, and it sounds like his mom is asking him to take on responsibilities that are a lot for a 10-year-old." Annie adds, "And I wonder, if there's not a lot of money, if he might not be getting enough to eat. I guess it's not much wonder that he's acting out. I probably would too!"

As an EA, you will have these bad days and, if you are fortunate, you will have a mentor like Bashir to help you gain perspective on children's behaviours. Your mentor might remind you that every child has a story to tell, and that listening to that story will help you to understand and decide how to respond.

Sometimes it seems like the odds are stacked against children like Stephen—or Sabrina or Ahmed, for that matter. But like all students, they have strengths and the right to develop to their full potential. As an EA, you have the opportunity to discover those strengths and help guide your students to overcome the obstacles that stand in the way of their success and happiness.

## Behaviour as Communication

In the story above, Bashir and Annie were wise to see Stephen's behaviour as a message that something was wrong in his life. Children find many ways to communicate the pain and vulnerability they are feeling. Perhaps Annie was a person Stephen felt he could trust with those feelings.

The same may be true of the other students Annie mentions. When Sabrina had her math meltdown, she might have been expressing her frustration with a task that was too difficult for her and made her feel inadequate compared to her classmates. Similarly, Ahmed may have decided that he was incapable of reading and has simply given up.

Perceptive EAs will quickly look beyond challenging behaviours to the underlying messages. No child likes to be out of control; the behaviours are a signal that something is not right in the child's world. If we see negative behaviour as communication, we quickly realize that it isn't meant to irritate us but is simply the desperate action of a child who can't cope with the conditions and expectations in their life.

The children to whom EAs are assigned often have behaviours that are quite challenging. They may be suffering from trauma due to exposure to violence, struggling with a learning disability that makes schoolwork frustrating, or living with a communication disorder that makes it difficult for them to connect with others. They might be functioning at a developmental stage that is quite different from their chronological age or have severe physical exceptionalities. Their home situation might be stressful. Because each child is different, they may require different responses to their behaviours. No strategy will work in every situation, and some situations require a variety of strategies.

## Behaviour Challenges and Trauma

In Chapter 8, we considered the effect of trauma and toxic stress on children. We'll revisit this topic now as it applies to guiding behaviours.

Children who have been traumatized are quite likely to exhibit challenging behaviours. Unless you understand the effects of trauma, these behaviours may leave you feeling resentful, frustrated, or angry. You may find yourself responding in ways that actually increase the child's trauma.

Trauma—whether it be one large traumatic event or many small stressful events that accumulate over time—can be overwhelming to children and affect every aspect of their intellectual, emotional, physical, and behavioural functioning (Poole, Talbot & Nathoo, 2017).

As we saw in Chapter 8, and according to the Child Welfare Information Gateway (2014), some of the effects of trauma on behaviour include:

- Lack of impulse control
- Distrusting or disobeying adults
- Fighting
- Aggression
- Running away
- Dissociating (feeling disconnected from reality)
- Substance abuse
- Suicide

Challenging behaviours are the child's way of responding to a world that they have experienced as unsafe and threatening. In the absence of reassuring relationships with adults, they have concluded that they are on their own and that no one will protect them.

It's useful to know, too, that if a child is acting in a way that seems extreme or unrelated to the reality of a situation, it could be that the child has been triggered by some aspect of the situation that reminds them of a previous trauma. Triggering can happen to you as well, if you have experienced stress or trauma in the past. This is one situation where self-awareness is critical for the EA. Being aware of your own triggers and of how to cope is critical to being able to respond to a child's stress or trauma without your own emotions taking over.

The Child Welfare Information Gateway (2014) offers these tips for working with children who have experienced trauma:

- Identify trauma triggers.
- Be emotionally and physically available even when the child acts in ways that keep adults at a distance.
- Be calm. Intense reactions may trigger a child who is already feeling overwhelmed.
- Don't take the child's behaviour personally.
- Listen.
- Be consistent and predictable.
- Allow the child some control.
- Build the child's self-esteem by providing opportunities for success.
- Set reasonable, consistent limits.

## Learning to Effectively Guide Behaviour

To effectively guide children's behaviour, you need basic knowledge of child development, an understanding of trauma, self-awareness, and the ability to observe and sensitively adapt to the needs of individual children.

You also need a stockpile of different options to choose from when dealing with a particular situation. Every child is different, and guiding behaviour in one child may require a different method or methods than in another. Whatever methods you use should have the following qualities: show respect and caring for the child; teach self-regulation of emotions; and help build a safe, positive, and accepting classroom environment.

Building a relationship with and learning about a child is the first step to guiding their behaviour in a positive manner. Having a trusting relationship is not a guarantee that the child won't act out with you; in fact, as we saw with Stephen in the story above, a child may be more likely to act out with you if you have a trusting relationship because the child feels safe with you. They feel you might really understand what is happening for them. However, having a personal connection with them and knowing the context for their behaviour can help you understand it and respond in a professional and appropriate manner.

## Preventing Challenging Behaviours

Prevention begins with creating an environment that promotes positive behaviour. EAs are often assigned to support children whose physical, mental, and emotional capacities set them apart as different, so one consideration in encouraging their positive behaviour is always to find ways to help them feel a sense of belonging.

The classroom environment has an important role in creating a sense of belonging for all students. A classroom that promotes belonging:
- Should be a calm, comfortable place where children can move around and engage with others
- Should not isolate children with exceptionalities or group these children exclusively together with other children with exceptionalities
- Should have pictures and books that show people of various cultures, races, and abilities, particularly those that are represented in the classroom
- Should make resources and materials available at a range of reading levels
- Should post a daily schedule or agenda in the room so children can anticipate what comes next

Consider factors in the classroom and the school that might be stressful for the child: Perhaps the level of activity is overwhelming, the noise level too loud, or the light too bright. School lockdown drills can be highly stressful experiences for children. To deal with stresses that may not be avoidable, some classrooms have a comfortable area with pillows, blankets, books, stuffed animals, and squeezable stress balls that children can retreat to when they need a calming environment. Materials from nature such as plants, animals (allergies permitting), pinecones, tree cookies, or sensory materials like bubble wrap and squares of fabric also have a calming effect. Soft music or nature sounds may contribute to a peaceful environment. For some students, wearing noise cancelling headphones is a useful way to block out classroom noise.

The way adults interact with children can also prompt trauma. EAs who are stressed or lack appropriate communication skills may respond to children with sarcasm, impatience, or a harsh voice. Personal awareness and the ability to manage one's own responses are required to support children experiencing trauma, and to positively guide behaviour.

# A Guidance Continuum

Our ultimate goal for all children is that they learn to regulate their own behaviour—that is, that they learn to behave appropriately without our intervention. One way to do this is to let them have as much control as possible in guidance situations.

Mary Lynne Matheson, our colleague and an instructor at NorQuest College in Edmonton, Alberta, has developed a continuum approach to guidance that progresses from the most to the least amount of control for the child. Appendix E shows her continuum framework (published here with her permission) for responding to children when the adult has concerns about their behaviour. In this framework, the EA or other adult begins with strategies that are as far to the top as possible (i.e., gives the child the greatest amount of control) then moves further down (i.e., lessening the amount of control allowed to the child) as needed.

## Guidance Strategies

This section explains some guidance strategies along the guidance continuum you might use when you are concerned about a child's behaviour. It begins with the strategies that are the most child-directed (i.e., top of the continuum), and ends with those that are the most adult-directed (i.e., at the bottom).

### Ignore behaviour

Sometimes it's best to ignore negative behaviour as long as it isn't unsafe for the child or others and doesn't destroy classroom materials. Be sure to give some positive attention when the behaviour ends.

> Alex keeps drumming his fingers on his desk while you are reading to him. It's annoying, but you don't respond. Eventually he stops and this is an opportunity for you to tell him that you've enjoyed having a chance to read with him.

### Natural consequence

If a child wants to do something that the adult feels is unwise but is not harmful to the child or others, the adult could let the child go ahead with the plan and discover the consequences.

> Annaliese refuses to wear mittens outside even though you worry that she'll be cold. You allow her to go outside without mittens but monitor closely and have mittens handy just in case.

### Proximity

A strategy that is very low in teacher control is simply to come and stand by the child or children. Even a thumbs up or eye contact from across the room can let children know the EA is watching. The proximity of the EA prompts the student to regulate their own behaviour. Remember, though, that your body language and facial expression are important here. Scowling or placing your hands on your hips might send a message of disapproval or exasperation rather than support.

> Reid and Antoine are working on a math task together when an argument breaks out between them. You move near to where they are working but don't intervene. The boys, probably aware of your presence, solve the problem on their own.

### Cue

One or two words can alert a child to an action they have missed or remind them of a desired behaviour. Tone of voice is important here as the cue needs to come across as a gentle reminder rather than an admonishment.

> As Jan comes in for recess, he drops his coat on the floor and doesn't stop to hang it up. You catch his eye, smile, and say, "your coat," in a pleasant voice. He returns to his locker and carefully hangs it up.

### Describe behaviour

Describing a problematic behaviour can alert the child to a problem and to the fact that you are paying attention to the problem.

> Three students are assigned to work on a project. Sam and Juno are busy brainstorming ideas, but Nikola is climbing around under his desk. You say pleasantly, "Nikola, I see that Sam and Juno have started on the project and you're underneath your desk."

### "I" messages

An "I" message describes the behaviour and tells the student what your concerns are about their behaviour. This gives the student an opportunity to be responsible for changing their behaviour. Also, providing information about the reason for your concern gives the child an opportunity to learn for another time.

> Jan drops his coat on the floor instead of hanging it in his locker. You say, "Jan, I'm worried that someone might trip on your coat when it's lying on the floor." When he doesn't respond, you follow up with another "I" message, "I'm also worried that it will get dirty or wet lying on the floor."

### Turn it back to the child

Take advantage of every opportunity to help children become self-directed problem-solvers.

> You notice that some of the sports equipment you've been using in gym is consistently not being put away. You say, "I notice that often some of the sports equipment is left out in the gym at the end of the class. What can we do to make sure that it gets put away every day?"

### Choices

Choices are a little more adult-directed. The task is nonnegotiable but the choice still gives the child some amount of self-determination.

> Peter dislikes math and stubbornly resists doing the worksheets the teacher has assigned. You give him a choice: "Peter, would you like to do the worksheets now or right after we get back from the library?"

> A four-year-old doesn't want to get dressed to go outside at playtime. The EA asks, "Would you like to wear your sweater or your jacket?"

It's important that the choices be offered in a pleasant manner and that they are real choices. Asking, for example, "Do you want to stop yelling or go to the principal's office?" comes across not as a choice but as an ultimatum.

### Contingency

A contingency often uses the words *as soon as*, *if*, or *when*.

> At the end of the day, the children have an opportunity to tell and/or show their classmates the work they have been doing that day. Arabella, seated with the others on the rug, is straining to get her hand up as high as possible, saying, "I want to! I want to!" The adult says, "Yes! You can show yours, Arabella, just as soon as Paul's had his turn."

A contingency is very useful. It can turn a *no*—no one likes to be told *no*—into a yes!

> Sami has finished his lunch and is ready to go outside to play. "Can I go out now?" he asks Jeff, the supervising EA. "Yes, of course! As soon as you put your lunch box away, out you go!"

### Word positively

Let children know what they *can* do rather than what they cannot do.

> When Bashir finishes reading his library book, he tosses it on the ground and begins another activity. Instead of telling Bashir not to throw his book on the floor, his EA says, "The book goes on the shelf."

### Logical consequences

A logical consequence is similar to a natural consequence except that the consequence is constructed by the adult. To be effective, logical consequences must be relevant to the problem, reasonable, and implemented in a respectful manner.

> An EA tells students who were pushing and shoving in a lineup to go to the back of the line.

> A student knocks over a display that another child is making.
> The EA guides the child to help reassemble the display and fix
> a piece that is broken.

### Roadblocks

Roadblocks are statements that shut down communication. They are adult-directed and don't help children to develop the skills to deal with problems or regulate their behaviour (see Chapter 7). In a busy classroom, EAs are managing many responsibilities at once. When a child asks you why they have to put their supplies away, it may be tempting to respond with, "Because I told you to!" This response puts up a roadblock. It is a response that leverages power over the child; it doesn't respect or teach them.

Of course, there are situations where using a roadblock—for instance, saying *no*, *stop*, or *don't*—may be the only alternative. If a child's actions are placing themselves or others in danger, you might need to respond immediately with a verbal command or even by physically removing the child.

### Time away

Time away involves offering a frustrated or distressed child a quiet, comfortable space within the classroom where they can sit and do something calming like read a book or cuddle a stuffed animal. The child should have control over when they feel calm enough to rejoin the group; adult support can be useful in helping them resume the activity that they left.

Time away is an effective strategy for teaching children to regulate their behaviour and emotions. In time, they can learn to remove themselves when they are feeling overwhelmed. However, in children who have experienced trauma, time away or timeout can feel like a rejection.

### Timeout

Timeout is the most adult-controlled of the behaviour strategies we've discussed so far. It refers to a behaviour management strategy wherein a child who is misbehaving is removed from an activity for a short period of time. It is intended to reduce the frequency of the challenging behaviour.

The practice of timeout is controversial. Critics point out that it doesn't teach the child positive behaviour and that it has the effect of confirming to the child and the child's peers that the child in timeout is "bad." As we know, a child will behave in accordance with their image of themselves, so timeout may ultimately increase challenging behaviours.

Provinces and individual jurisdictions have guidelines outlining if and how timeout may be used in schools. In Alberta, for example, timeout is to be used only in accordance with established policies and procedures, and only as a last resort after positive and proactive management strategies have failed. Timeout should only be given by knowledgeable and skilled staff.

## Using the Guidance Continuum

The guidance continuum that we have discussed moves from the least adult-directed to the most adult-directed guidance approaches. Generally speaking, unless there is a clear and imminent danger, the EA would begin with the least adult-directed approach—the one that gives the child the most control. Then, if that doesn't work, the EA would gradually move to more and more adult-directed approaches. Here is an example of how that might work:

> The EA, Maxine, notices that Ethan and Henry are having heated words on the playground. She moves over to stand close to them, but the disagreement progresses to pushes as the boys shout, "You cheated!" and, "You're lying!"
>
> Maxine moves between them and says, "It sounds like there's a problem here. Who would like to tell me what's happening?"
>
> The boys begin to both talk at once, at which point Maxine says, "I can only listen to one person at a time. Ethan, why don't you go first and then you can go next, Henry. I promise I will listen to each of you."
>
> The boys state their grievances and Maxine invites them to problem-solve. They arrive at a solution. A few minutes later, however, Ethan pushes Henry to the ground.
>
> Maxine realizes that the natural consequence of their disagreement will be that someone gets hurt, so this approach would be inappropriate in this case. She decides that offering choices might not be effective, so she moves to a contingency. She separates the boys and sends each to a different corner of the schoolyard. "When you can be together without fighting, you can play together again."

This example shows the guidance continuum in operation as Maxine moves from child-directed to adult-directed approaches. What is not shown in this example is the degree to which Maxine would also have given attention to discovering what is at the root of the boys' antipathy. Is this an ongoing pattern, or are they usually friends? Has either of them experienced recent problems at school or at home? Are there dynamics in the class or school that are playing into the dispute? Perhaps, in other words,

Ethan and Henry's schoolyard fight is an indication of a problem or problems that need further attention.

### Active listening

In Chapter 7, we discussed the importance of listening to a child's strong emotions. *Active listening* is a way to acknowledge children's feelings, desires, and thoughts, and let them know that you understand. Regardless of the guidance strategy you are using, be sure to switch to active listening if the child is upset or expresses strong negative emotion.

For example, if you offer a student a choice and they say, "I won't do any of your stupid choices," you should actively listen to the child's strong emotions. You might say, "You really don't like my choices, do you?" and listen closely to the child's response. Once the child feels understood, they may be ready to problem-solve with you to find a solution that works for both of you.

In the example below, active listening helps two children to solve a dispute.

> Suzanne and Ariel are developing a skit to perform for the class. Ariel, visibly upset, complains to Chris, the EA, that Suzanne won't listen to any of her ideas.
>
> Chris listens attentively, using body language and minimal encouragers (nodding, "mm-hmm") to show Ariel that he is taking her concern and her emotions seriously.
>
> Suzanne approaches with her own complaint that Ariel wants to introduce a role that doesn't fit in the story. Chris listens attentively to her as well.
>
> Chris paraphrases the problem: "Ariel, you're upset because you feel like Suzanne isn't listening to your ideas. Suzanne, you don't feel that the princess role fits in the story. Am I right?" Both children nod. "This is a problem," Chris goes on. "What do you think you can do to solve it?"
>
> The girls discuss, each reaffirming their own views but more calmly, and eventually they decide that perhaps the princess could be the narrator. Chris restates their solution, checking with each to see if they are in agreement. Later Chris checks in again, just to make sure that everything is still going well.

Initially, emotions were running high, but Chris managed to defuse them by listening carefully to each child's side of the situation. This allowed the children to move on to problem-solving and come to a solution. Eventually, they will learn how to work through these situations on their own.

## Seclusion and Physical Restraint

Seclusion refers to the involuntary confinement of a child in a locked area from which the child cannot leave. Sometimes it is associated with physical restraint, as restraint may be involved in moving the child to the seclusion area. It is important to note that seclusion and physical restraint are *not* procedures for managing behaviour; they are crisis intervention measures. If they are used, it is because a child's behaviour is placing the child or others in imminent danger of serious physical harm and all positive guidance strategies have failed. They are not to be used as discipline or to force a child to comply.

Provinces and school jurisdictions vary with respect to regulations about the use of seclusion and physical restraints in schools. Generally speaking, these measures must be used only as part of a comprehensive behaviour management plan, the parents or guardians must be involved in the formulation of the plan, and the staff must be trained in the proper administration of these measures. In most cases, the EA will be the person responsible for implementing the plan.

Seclusion rooms must be comfortable and the child must be fully visible to staff while in the room. Seclusion and/or restraint are implemented only in an emergency and must be discontinued when there is no longer a threat. Any situations where seclusion or restraint are employed must be thoroughly documented and reviewed as soon as possible after the incident.

The effects of seclusion and physical restraint can be far-reaching; for example, seclusion rooms are often located beside the school office so that office staff can oversee the safety of the child. Imagine the feelings of other children and staff when a furious child is being forcibly propelled, kicking and screaming, down the school hallway. Imagine, also, the feelings of the child themselves and the EA. Such an environment is not one in which people can feel safe, and it is likely to trigger trauma responses in those who are vulnerable. Obviously, seclusion and physical restraint are used only in emergencies, if at all, because of the possible physical and psychological damage to the child, the EA, and other children and staff.

How you respond to children's challenging behaviours can have a huge effect on their behaviour and on the classroom environment. In Chapter 13, we will consider an essential skill for EAs: the ability to observe and document behaviour.

## Takeaways

- When children misbehave, they are telling you that something isn't right in their world.
- Children who have experienced trauma or toxic stress are very likely to have challenging behaviours. They need a calm, reassuring adult to help them through difficult times.
- Because we want children to develop skills for self-regulation and problem-solving, we use the least amount of intervention required to redirect their behaviour.
- A guidance continuum guides us in moving from interventions that give children greater control to those that require adults to have greater control.
- Seclusion and physical restraint are not guidance strategies but crisis intervention methods. They should only be used when all other methods have failed and the child's behaviour risks causing serious harm to the child or others.

## Reflection and Discussion

- What are your expectations for children's behaviour? Are there child behaviours that might trigger you to respond in ways that you'd prefer not to?
- Think about a time you were disciplined as a child for something you did. What feelings did you experience at that time? What do you think about the experience now? What did you learn? Might there have been another way for the adult to have handled the situation?
- Think of ways you have used, or have seen others use, to guide behaviour. To what extent were they child-directed or adult-directed? Where would they fit on the guidance continuum?

# Observing and Documenting

*I think that my job is to observe people and the world, and not to judge them. I always hope to position myself away from so-called conclusions. I would like to leave everything wide open to all the possibilities in the world.*

—HARUKI MURAKAMI

## Learning Outcomes

After reading this chapter, you will be able to answer these questions:
- What kinds of information can you gather through observation?
- Why is it important that, as an EA, you be a skilled observer?
- What are some different kinds of observations and when might you use them?
- What are the important things to remember about writing observations?

## Introduction

As an EA, you will be in a position to observe children at times and in ways that the teacher is unable to. Your observations will guide your own interactions and decisions with children and will provide valuable information to the teacher and other team members. In this chapter, you will learn about many different kinds of observation that you can do in order to get useful information and use it appropriately.

> When Francine, an EA, meets with her mentor teacher, she brings a sheaf of observations that she has written about

various children over the last week. The teacher reads these carefully and discusses them with Francine. They become the basis for some of the planning for the following week.

Francine has noticed that on three occasions, Chelsea has ventured over to Khalid and watched what he was doing with his communication board. Francine and her mentor teacher decide to try pairing Chelsea and Khalid for a task on Monday while providing the necessary support for them to communicate effectively.

Francine has also observed that Soe was able to read all of her classmates' names from the job chart. They decide to ask Soe if she would like to match the names to classroom jobs when they are assigned on Monday.

Arashdeep, Francine has noticed, has been talking excitedly about his family's recent trip to the space museum. Perhaps, they think, he'd like to write about this trip and present it to the class.

In a classroom where the teacher is responsible for the learning and development of 26 children, Francine's input is a huge asset in helping to support each child.

Her observations show:

- What individual children know and can do
- Children's interests and what they enjoy
- The relationships and dynamics that exist within the group
- What specific learning needs should be addressed
- The state of the children's wellbeing
- Any puzzling situations that might require further observation

The observations help both Francine and the teacher get to know the children better. They become a basis for discussion and planning—in this case with the mentor teacher, but sometimes with consultants and families, too.

## What Does It Mean to Observe?

There are many different ways to make and record observations. Perhaps you are passing by a table where two children are working and notice an interesting and possibly significant interaction. You make a note on a slip of paper, keep it to discuss with the teacher, and include it in the child's file. Maybe you are interested in learning more about a child's particular behaviour, so you watch carefully and make a note of the times and circumstances when the behaviour occurs. Perhaps you've been asked to assess a child's large motor skills and have been given a checklist to complete.

Your approach to observation will depend upon your reason for observing. Using a range of approaches will help you build a holistic picture of a child.

## Approaches to Observation

### Anecdotal observations

Anecdotal observations are recorded after the event has occurred and are written in the past tense. Anecdotal records should focus on what is significant and include important details in the sequence in which they occurred. They should include what the child said and did, body language, tone of voice, and other relevant details. The aim is to give as complete a picture as possible. This is probably the kind of observation that you will use most often.

> Marika played alone in the snow fort for about five minutes, sitting on her knees, patting at the snowballs with both hands and talking to herself. When Evelyn approached, she looked up at her and said, "Our house is almost finished." Evelyn smiled and knelt beside Marika, where they continued to pat at the snowballs and chat.

### Running observations

Running observations are recorded in the present tense while the action is occurring, and provide a more detailed account of a child's behaviour. It is useful to include the time period in which the observation occurs, or to record the time in intervals.

> 9:30-9:35: Henry (age nine) is in the library during shared reading time. He is sitting with a grade 1 student on the floor in the rug area. He is sitting cross-legged and holding a closed book, *The Little Red Hen*, on his knees. He opens the book to the first page and holds it up and to his left so that the pictures face the grade 1 student. He begins to read with expression, then stops to ask the student if she can see. When she says, "Yes," he resumes reading. He stops to ask if she knows what the word "kernel" means. She replies that it's a seed and he nods. He proceeds to read to the end of the book.

### Sociograms

A sociogram is a map of the interactions among a group of children over a designated period of time. The sociogram below shows that Elena had interactions with a number of children while Melia may have been excluded from the group.

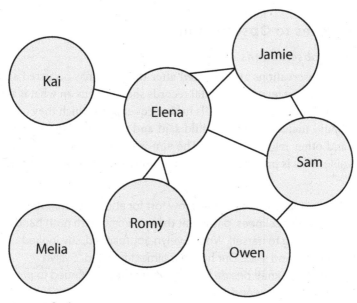

**FIGURE 13.1. Sociogram**

### Time samples

Time samples are a record of the number of times a particular behaviour occurs over the course of a day. They help show why and when a particular behaviour tends to occur and whether it is increasing or decreasing in frequency.

| Liam hit other students five times today.

### Event samples

In event sampling, the observer records an event every time it happens. The observation includes the actions or events that occurred immediately before the behaviour in question, the behaviour itself, and the consequences. Event samples help to show what has provoked a certain behaviour and help in finding strategies to manage it.

Monday:
**What happens to cause the behaviour:** Damian is working diligently on his drawing. Wilma (teacher) tells the class that it's time to clean up for the gym.
**Behaviour observed:** Damian looks up with an angry expression and sweeps his papers to the floor.
**Consequence:** Wilma tells Damian that he can't come to the gym until his papers are picked up. Gerry (EA) stays with him in the room while the other children go to the gym with the teacher. Damian sits at his desk, frowning.
Tuesday:
**What happens to cause the behaviour:** Repeat of yesterday
**Behaviour observed:** Damian shouts, "I haven't finished!" and throws his pencil on the floor.
**Consequence:** Gerry asks, "Would you like me to put your drawing on the art shelf so you can finish it when you come back?" Damian replies, "I don't want to go to the gym." Gerry asks, "What is it you don't like about the gym?" Damian says, "I don't like to run. It hurts my legs." Gerry suggests that he will walk with Damian around the edge of the gym and Damian agrees.

### Photographs

Photographs can provide an excellent record of a child's abilities and accomplishments. Photographs taken over time can provide a record of development.

### Work samples

Collecting samples of children's work throughout the year is a good way to assess their progress and to show their progress to them and their families.

## Observation Basics

Whatever kind of observation you are using, it's important that you only write what you are seeing and hearing, but that you do so with as much detail as possible. You can devise your own shorthand and transcribe these notes later if necessary. You may include drawings in your notes, as well. Stick figures, for example, are useful for portraying difficult-to-describe body positions.

The observation needs to be as objective as possible, without judgement or evaluation. The word you use should be descriptive but should not convey any bias.

> **Say this:** Sara puts the crown on her head, looks in the mirror, and smiles.
> **Not this:** Sarah is happy with how she looks in the crown.
> **Say this:** Russell stands by the door with his head down and a sad expression.
> **Not this:** Russell stands sulking by the door.

Finally, know that your presence will influence what is happening, so be as unobtrusive as possible.

## Interpreting Your Observations

As you are reviewing your observations, ask yourself these questions:

- What developmental skills do these observations identify?
- What ideas and questions are children exploring?
- What changes am I noticing over time?
- What strengths and challenges are apparent?
- How might this information be used to plan future experiences and interactions?

So far in this book, you've learned important skills to take into your career as an EA. In the last chapter, current and retired EAs will offer you advice based on their own years of experience in schools. Finally, you will consider how to stay healthy in order to bring your best self to the valuable work you do with students.

## Takeaways

- Observation is an essential skill for you as an EA. It allows you to get to know students better and provide teachers, consultants, and families with valuable information.
- There are many different methods of making and recording observations. The method you choose in any given situation will depend on the purpose of the observation.
- Observations need to be objective, detailed, and free of bias. They should include only what you see and hear at that time, and not your interpretations of those observations.

## Reflection and Discussion

- Of the observation methods that you've studied, which do you feel might be especially useful in your day-to-day work?
- How might you change each of the following statements to eliminate judgement or bias?
  › Ana, age 14, has dirty blond hair and blue eyes. She is sloppily dressed.
  › As usual, Jason is preoccupied with his Lego construction.
  › Ilianna has made a beautiful drawing.

## 14

# Surviving and Thriving

*In times of stress, the best thing we can do for
each other is to listen with our ears and our
hearts and to be assured that our questions
are just as important as our answers.*

—*FRED ROGERS*

### Learning Outcomes

After reading this chapter, you will be able to answer these questions:

- What are some tips from experienced EAs that you would especially like to keep in mind?
- What are some signs that you are overly stressed?
- What are ways that you can look after your physical and emotional health?

## Introduction

Some of you will be familiar with Fred Rogers, the host of the popular children's television show *Mister Rogers' Neighborhood* for over 30 years. He sent a message of caring and hope to young viewers and helped them deal with difficult emotions such as anger and sadness. From the cozy confines of his imaginary neighbourhood, he spoke of trust, courage, love, and honesty. Famously, he would sign off with this message: "You've made this day a special day by just your being you. There is no person in the whole world like you, and I like you just the way you are" (Rogers, 1968).

Tales abound of the lives Fred Rogers influenced, if not saved. Merritt (2018) recounts the story of a child with profound autism who spoke for the first time when watching *Mister Rogers,* and began to make eye contact with his father one day when he said, "Let's go to the Neighborhood of Make-Believe" (one of the settings on the show). The child went on to learn to speak and read; his father travelled to thank Fred Rogers personally.

As an EA, you may not have Fred Rogers' ability or opportunity to reach out to millions of viewers, but you can make a profound difference in the lives of the children in your own life and work. The job that you do is tremendously important. At the same time, it can also be stressful and exhausting.

## Voices from the Field

Some days will be hard, and you'll have to remind yourself of the beliefs, hopes, and values that brought you into the profession. Other days will be so rewarding that they will carry you through some of the more frustrating times.

> I remember when I first started working with Julia. She was in grade 3 and still not catching on to reading. The consultant said we should give up and let her learn auditorily. But I kept working with her and she started catching on. She was so excited to be making progress. Her mom cried the first time Julia read to her. It was so satisfying to be able to make this difference in their lives.
>
> *—LYNN, A RETIRED EA*

> It's exciting to see the joy in their eyes and the surprise on their face when they finally figure out that they're able to do something.
>
> *—JANICE, AN EA*

## Tips from the Pros

We asked a group of experienced EAs what advice they would give to EAs starting out in their careers. Here is a summary of their responses.

### Work with teachers

- Observe the teacher. Get to know the teacher's style of teaching, classroom management strategies, and teaching philosophy.
- Ask the teacher what they expect of you.
- Use your initiative but don't overstep. Make suggestions and, with the teacher's permission, experiment with new ideas.

- Be flexible. Be willing to change your plans if necessary. Adapt to the teacher's needs.
- Keep your eyes open for opportunities to help.

### Work with students

- Be willing to adapt your activities to meet each student's needs.
- Get to know each student well. Learn about their unique background and capabilities.
- Use the same classroom behaviour management systems as the teacher to ensure consistency for the students.
- Truly appreciate the strengths that each child brings.

### Communicate

- Be able to communicate clearly and adapt your communication style to different situations.

### Be professional

- Research your school's policies and curriculum so you can answer questions accurately and know what to do in case of extraordinary circumstances or events.
- Never pull out your phone on school time. If there is an emergency, the call can go through the school.
- In most cases, it's best that your first job not be in your own children's school.

### Grow as a professional

- Advocate for EA professional development activities. Get every bit of training that's offered to you. The more training you have, the more opportunities you have.
- Learn from other staff. Observe what works and what doesn't.
- Recess is a good time to make observations and connections. You can learn a lot at recess if you aren't on your phone.
- Be familiar with your union and your rights.

### Stay positive and healthy

- Put on a smile!
- A sense of humour is a tremendous asset.
- Self-care is very important. You really have to look after yourself; if you aren't looking after yourself, you won't have anything left to offer your work.

# Looking After Yourself

The intensity of working with children can be stressful, and being overly stressed can have serious physical and emotional effects. Some signs of stress are:

- Not sleeping well
- Often feeling tired
- Feeling overwhelmed or constantly worried
- Decreased energy
- Losing interest in activities you used to enjoy
- Having frequent headaches, bodily pain, or other physical problems
- Gaining or losing weight
- Feeling irritable or worried
- Having difficulty concentrating
- Using tobacco, alcohol, or other drugs to relieve stress

It is impossible to avoid stress completely, but you can find ways to reduce unnecessary stress and deal with the stresses you do have in your life in healthy ways.

### Exercise

Exercising might feel like the last thing you want to do at the end of an exhausting day with children. However, it is an effective way to combat stress. Research shows that exercise reduces stress hormones such as cortisol, and helps to release endorphins, the chemicals that increase feelings of wellbeing. Regular exercise can improve sleep quality and can help you to feel more physically and emotionally confident, which can in turn increase your mental wellbeing.

### Journal

Keeping a journal can help relieve stress and anxiety. You can write down what you are stressed about or use the journal to record and remind you of things you are grateful for in your life and work.

### Build support networks

Build networks of support both inside and outside of work. Your professional connections can help you solve problems or gain new perspectives on work situations. Confidentiality considerations mean that you can't take your work situations to your social supports; this can be a good reminder that your work is just one part of your life. Having strong social ties outside of work can help you gain perspective, weather stressful times, and lower your anxiety levels. Belonging to a club, singing in a choir, or being part of a sports team all have the benefit of connecting you to other people.

### Laugh

Laughter has been found to have a positive effect on many organs, including your heart, lungs, and muscles. It has also been shown to increase endorphin levels. Laughter relieves your stress response, decreasing heart rate and blood pressure. It can relax your muscles and stimulate circulation. The Mayo Clinic (2019) adds that, over the long term, laughter can improve your immune system, relieve pain, help you cope with difficult situations, connect with people, and fight depression and anxiety. These are good reasons to find the humour in everyday life and seek out people and experiences that make you laugh.

### Learn to say no

Take control over the parts of your life that you can change by not taking on more than you can handle. Consider that for every new thing you take on, there may be one or more things that you have to let go: choose wisely. When you don't have a lot of control over what you do, as when you are being assigned jobs at work, saying yes with a caveat may be a useful approach: "Yes, I'll help with that just as soon as I get Jamie dressed." This approach requires that you be good at identifying priorities, but it also communicates to you and others that you can only do one thing at a time and can help you to keep from feeling overwhelmed.

### Avoid procrastinating

Leaving things to the last minute adds to stress. Make a to-do list organized by priorities and give yourself realistic deadlines to work through that list. Be sure to add enough time for the unexpected demands that may well arise.

### Touch

Positive touch, whether cuddling with your child, your partner, or your puppy, has been found to foster the release of oxytocin—a hormone associated with love and bonding—and lower blood pressure.

### Listen to music

Listening to calming music or nature sounds can be soothing, but listening to any music that you like can be beneficial.

### Breathe

Deep breathing activates a relaxation response. There are various methods for learning to breathe deeply. Practices that focus on body and breath awareness such as yoga, Pilates, and meditation, have been found to be effective ways to relieve stress.

*Have a good cry*
Crying can be a good release.

---

EAs may be at particular risk for secondary traumatic stress (STS), or compassion fatigue, because of their close engagement with children who have been traumatized. STS is a form of physical and emotional burnout and exhaustion. If you are doing everything possible to reduce your stress but are still feeling vulnerable, don't hesitate to seek help.

## Supporting Inclusion in a Diverse Society

We began this book by describing a typical Canadian classroom. In this classroom, the children come from diverse family backgrounds. Some families are newcomers to Canada, while others—Indigenous families—have occupied these lands for many thousands of years. Some families are headed by a lone parent, others by two parents. One child lives with his grandparents, and another with a foster family. Some families have same-sex parents and one child has a parent who is transitioning from male to female. While some families have a comfortable income, others struggle. The families speak various languages and belong to different religious groups. This is the diversity of Canadian society in the twenty-first century.

In addition to the diversity that the children bring to the classroom by virtue of their family backgrounds, there is a huge range of abilities, interests, and needs among the children themselves. There is a child who is an enthusiastic writer and another who is a gifted mathematician. Others struggle with academics. One child has autism, while another has challenging behaviour issues. One prefers painting as a means of expression, another likes gymnastics. Two children who are newcomers to Canada are just beginning to fit in at recess. There are children who stand out for their sense of responsibility and the depth of their caring and passions.

In a diverse and inclusive society, each of these children has a right to an educational experience where they can have feelings of success, belonging, and worthiness. We hope that, having worked through this book, you will understand both the complexity of this task and some of the ways that you, as an EA, can help to make it happen.

Always remember that your work as an EA is vitally important to the children you support. Your involvement can mean the difference for them between a good day and a bad day; between feeling like a success or a failure, being included or rejected. Your caring and competence sow the seeds for a compassionate community that can acknowledge and benefit from the strengths that diversity offers.

The influence of an EA extends well beyond the classroom. By sowing the seeds of inclusion in your work with children, you are helping to grow a society where everyone is appreciated and can contribute. The work of an EA is a big responsibility, but also an incredible opportunity.

## Takeaways

- Working as an EA is rewarding, important, busy, and sometimes stressful.
- You need to develop skills for working effectively with teachers, students, consultants, and families.
- Take advantage of opportunities to grow your skills and demonstrate professionalism.
- To do your best work, you need to look after yourself. This includes incorporating practices in your life that will help you to control your overall stress level.

## Reflection and Discussion

- Look back at Chapter 3, where you considered the skills, abilities, and beliefs that you will bring to working as an EA. Would you make any changes to your answers now that you have more information about the position?
- What are some of the skills you would like to develop at this point in order to make your work as an EA more effective? How do you plan to develop these skills?
- Where do you see your career as an EA in five years?
- Look at the epigraphs that begin each chapter. Which inspires you the most? Do you have another favourite quotation that inspires your work with children?

# Appendix A

# Inclusive Community Planning Matrix

|  | PERSONAL | SOCIAL | INTELLECTUAL |
|---|---|---|---|
| In elective classrooms |  |  |  |
| In content classrooms |  |  |  |
| In the school |  |  |  |
| Outside of the school |  |  |  |

*Note.* Moore (n.d.), printed with permission.

# Appendix B

# Individual Educational Plan (IEP) Template

Student: _____    Student ID: _____

School: _____

Teacher: _____    Principal: _____

Person responsible for the IEP: _____

### Student Profile

Current grade: _____

Birthdate: _____

Instruction: Adapted programming or modified curriculum

Identified exceptionalities: _____

### Student's Areas of Strengths and Needs
(identified by parent/guardian, teacher, and EA)

| AREAS OF STRENGTH | AREAS OF NEED |
|---|---|
|  |  |
|  |  |
|  |  |
|  |  |

## Accommodations for Learning
(including assistive and adaptive technology)

| INSTRUCTIONAL ACCOMMODATIONS | ENVIRONMENTAL ACCOMMODATIONS | ASSESSMENT ACCOMMODATIONS |
|---|---|---|
|  |  |  |

## Human Resources
(teaching and non-teaching)

| NAME OF PERSON/ AGENCY | TYPE OF SUPPORT | FREQUENCY |
|---|---|---|
|  |  |  |

## Goals
(Refer to the areas of need identified above.
Make one academic and one behavioural or social goal.)

|  | TARGET DATE TO ACHIEVE GOAL | WHAT WILL THE STUDENT LEARN? | HOW WILL YOU KNOW THEY HAVE LEARNED IT? |
|---|---|---|---|
| Goal 1 (academic) |  |  |  |
| Goal 2 (behavioural/social) |  |  |  |

## Reviews

| Review 1<br>Date: | Goal | What the student has learned so far and how you know they have learned it |
|---|---|---|
| | 1. | |
| | 2. | |
| Review 2<br>Date: | | What the student has learned so far and how you know they have learned it |
| | 1. | |
| | 2. | |

## Final Review: Year End Summary
(Was the goal achieved? How do you know?)

| Goal 1 | |
|---|---|
| Goal 2 | |

# Transition Plan
(Consider transition between activities, classes, and grades.
Include cultural transitions.)

| Between activities | |
|---|---|
| Between classes | |
| Grade to grade | |
| Cultural and linguistic | |

# Signatures

| | INITIAL MEETING DATE: | REVIEW 1 DATE: | REVIEW 2 DATE: | FINAL REVIEW DATE: |
|---|---|---|---|---|
| Student (if applicable) | | | | |
| Parent/Guardian | | | | |
| Teacher | | | | |
| Educational Assistant | | | | |
| Principal | | | | |

# Appendix C

# Differentiating Instruction for Academic Learning

## COGNITIVE/NEUROLOGICAL NEEDS

| Gifted or talented | |
|---|---|
| CHARACTERISTICS | LEARNING SUPPORTS |
| • Shows exceptionally high capability in specific disciplines, intellect, or creativity<br>• Has areas of strength and weakness as well as interest and disinterest<br>• Often capable of learning more quickly and in more depth | • Use open-ended tasks and open questioning<br>• Begin with what they know about a given topic and build on that<br>• Use flexible groupings (e.g., grouping by ability or interest)<br>• Work on developing higher-order thinking skills (e.g., reflection, evaluation, prediction, exploration)<br>• Provide extra challenge through tiered assignments, online learning, self-directed research projects, or independent studies<br>• Give opportunities to work with external experts<br>• Encourage independence |

| Mild intellectual disability (MID) | |
|---|---|
| CHARACTERISTICS | LEARNING SUPPORTS |
| • Functions about 2 to 4 years below grade level<br>• Exceptionality tends to affect not only academic performance but also speech development, memory, and attention span | • Allow student to work at own pace, giving extra time when needed<br>• Model learning tasks<br>• Use wall charts, calendars, photos of an activity or day to reinforce structure and sequencing<br>• Break down tasks into smaller pieces<br>• Give immediate positive feedback<br>• Phrase questions simply and allow response time<br>• Use a range of multisensory approaches to teaching<br>• Ask open-ended questions which require a response beyond just *yes* or *no*<br>• Find alternate resources appropriate to student's level<br>• Allow student to present their work in various ways<br>• Encourage independence<br>• Reinforce target behaviours and new skills |
| Severe intellectual disability (SID) | |
| CHARACTERISTICS | LEARNING SUPPORTS |
| • Has greater limitations than MID in intellectual abilities and adaptive functioning<br>• Has difficulties focusing attention and getting information into memory<br>• Language may be delayed or may not develop | • Keep the theme as consistent as possible with the classroom curriculum<br>• Use concrete assignments broken into smaller tasks<br>• Provide models or examples of tasks<br>• Ask questions at the level of student's abilities<br>• Use the same materials as being used by the class but for different purposes<br>• Use simpler vocabulary<br>• Provide community-based experiences and tasks<br>• Reinforce target behaviours and new skills |

(continued on next page)

## COGNITIVE/NEUROLOGICAL NEEDS (*continued*)

### Autism spectrum disorders (ASDs)

| CHARACTERISTICS | LEARNING SUPPORTS |
|---|---|
| • Has social interaction and social communication deficits<br>• Different students with ASD have different levels of functioning and require very different levels of support | • Provide supportive peer partners<br>• Make use of the student's interests, strengths, talents, and skills wherever possible<br>• Encourage turn-taking activities; use circle time and social stories<br>• Give specific directions (e.g., how many lines of writing you want them to do)<br>• Give one instruction at a time and ask the student to repeat it back<br>• Keep the theme as consistent as possible with the rest of the class<br>• Use visual supports, technology-based instruction, and concrete representations of the content<br>• Give direct instruction at an appropriate level<br>• Maintain a consistent, organized space and materials with clear expectations<br>• Plan for transitions |

### Attention deficit disorder (ADD) and attention deficit hyperactivity disorder (ADHD)

| CHARACTERISTICS | LEARNING SUPPORTS |
|---|---|
| • A persistent pattern of inattention, impulsiveness, hyperactivity, or all of these | • Give clear instructions<br>• Repeat instructions<br>• Post a to do list and cross things off as accomplished<br>• Ensure adequate support at the beginning of a task then gradually fade out support<br>• Change type of activities and duration more frequently to retain attention |

## Learning disabilities (LDs)

| RANGE OF CHALLENGES | LEARNING SUPPORTS |
|---|---|
| • Discrepancy between ability and school achievement unrelated to either physical or emotional exceptionality or to environmental, cultural, or economic disadvantage<br>• Examples:<br>  › *Dyslexia*. Difficulty learning to read. Most common<br>  › *Dyscalculia*. Difficulty learning mathematics<br>  › *Dysgraphia*. Difficulty learning written expression | • Supports must occur in the context of the subject matter rather than isolated to specific skills<br>• Highlight main ideas<br>• Emphasize organizational skills, note-taking strategies<br>• Provide extra time to practice<br>• Check to ensure understanding and use of strategies |

## SOCIAL/EMOTIONAL/BEHAVIOURAL NEEDS

| CHARACTERISTICS | LEARNING SUPPORTS |
|---|---|
| • Interacts dysfunctionally with environment (e.g., classroom, home, community)<br>• May be related to experiences of trauma | • Ensure student knows the daily routine (a visual/picture schedule) at beginning of day and can refer to it throughout the day as needed<br>• Provide structure, predictability, and consistency<br>• Offer challenging, respectful, and cognitively engaging activities<br>• Provide immediate, frequent, and specific feedback<br>• Convey high expectations and support to be successful – model desired behaviours you expect<br>• Explicitly teach and practice coping/calming strategies – create a "calming spot"<br>• When dealing with conflict, use a calm, not angry, voice, and describe what happened in few words<br>• Brainstorm better "choices" with students<br>• Follow the student's behaviour support plan<br>• Use strategies to facilitate smooth transitions throughout the day<br>• Implement crisis response and de-escalation strategies |

(*continued on next page*)

## COMMUNICATION, SPEECH, AND LANGUAGE NEEDS

| RANGE OF CHALLENGES | LEARNING SUPPORTS |
| --- | --- |
| • Language delay<br>• Difficulty with receptive language<br>• Difficulty with expressive language<br>• Aphasia<br>• Apraxia<br>• Articulation<br>• Dysfluency<br>• Voice disorders<br>• Orofacial defects | • Model simple, clear speech<br>• Avoid speaking too quickly – slow your rate<br>• Listen patiently and don't interrupt; give time for the student to respond to questions<br>• Pair with a good peer language model and supportive classmates when appropriate<br>• Use props to encourage student to speak more (e.g., digital recorders, videos)<br>• Teach language skills through games (e.g., 20 questions and other games using verbal cues)<br>• Use sequencing and matching activities to develop language<br>• Support student use of alternative communication devices<br>• Provide the child opportunities to engage in conversations |

## ENGLISH LANGUAGE LEARNERS

| EXAMPLES | LEARNING SUPPORTS |
| --- | --- |
| • Indigenous students who speak an Indigenous language at home<br>• Students who arrive as immigrants from non-English-speaking countries<br>• Students born in Canada to parents who speak limited English | • Be warm and accepting<br>• Help student feel comfortable<br>• If possible, seat student near someone who speaks the same language<br>• Connect student with classmates you know will be welcoming<br>• Observe how student interacts with someone who understands their first language<br>• Use visual aids, gestures, and age-appropriate games and puzzles |

## SENSORY NEEDS

### Hearing

| EXAMPLES AND CHARACTERISTICS | LEARNING SUPPORTS |
|---|---|
| • Hearing needs may be loosely categorized as:<br>  › *Deafness.* Severe to profound deficits in ability to hear. May use American Sign Language (ASL) or alternate communication systems and may use hearing devices.<br>  › *Mild to moderate hearing loss.* Usually wear hearing devices.<br>• Speech and language development may be delayed. | • Check to make sure student is wearing their personal hearing equipment and FM system<br>• Ensure hearing devices are functioning well<br>• For optimal communication, ensure student has a direct line of sight to see the speaker's face (and upper body) for receptive communication<br>• Use preferential seating – make sure student is positioned with back to windows (so speaker is not in glare) and away from noise<br>• Listening is fatiguing; try to find ways to reduce need to listen (e.g., use visual aids, written summaries, manipulatives, notes, etc.)<br>• Break down tasks into understandable chunks<br>• Use levelled reading materials or controlled materials that support the gradual learning of new syntactic structures<br>• Preteach new vocabulary and concepts<br>• Provide opportunities for extra practice of new concepts<br>• Pair verbal instructions with written or visual instructions; repeat instructions frequently<br>• Avoid activities where student must close their eyes and imagine<br>• Use language experience approach, hands-on activities, graphic organizers, and manipulatives to enhance learning<br>• When reading aloud, include the name of the character speaking as student may otherwise find it difficult to follow<br>• Reinforce auditory, speech, and language skills |

*(continued on next page)*

## SENSORY NEEDS (*continued*)

### Vision

| CHARACTERISTICS | LEARNING SUPPORTS |
|---|---|
| • Visual acuity is not sufficient to participate easily in everyday activities<br>• May have delays in development because of limited experiences in their environment | • Use resources such as large-print books, braille books, adaptive and assistive technology<br>• Use enlarged text where appropriate, or use or create text audio recordings<br>• Adjust time for test-taking and homework; test student orally<br>• Don't rearrange the classroom without warning student<br>• Reduce glare on boards, desks, and other environmental objects<br>• Use strategies to support student orientation and mobility |

## CHRONIC HEALTH / MEDICAL NEEDS

| EXAMPLES | LEARNING SUPPORTS |
|---|---|
| • *Nervous system impairment.* Results from damage or dysfunction of the brain or spinal cord. Includes cerebral palsy, spina bifida, epilepsy, Tourette syndrome, brain injury, and fetal alcohol spectrum disorder (FASD)<br>• *Musculoskeletal conditions.* Includes muscular dystrophy and juvenile arthritis<br>• *Other chronic health conditions.* Diabetes, allergies, asthma, cystic fibrosis, Crohn's disease, ulcerative colitis, cancer, leukemia, and others | • Familiarize yourself with characteristics, emergency responses, and teaching strategies as needed<br>• Listen to student and their family to understand their cultural perspectives on student's condition<br>• Ensure accessibility in the classroom (e.g., safe movement for wheelchair users, materials where student can easily reach them)<br>• Student may miss a great deal of school because of their health and will need assistance in keeping up with the class<br>• Consider assistive and distance communication technologies where appropriate<br>• Take into account possible side effects of medication including tiredness, loss of concentration, or misbehaviour |

# Appendix D

# Differentiating Instruction for Social Learning

## COGNITIVE/NEUROLOGICAL NEEDS

| Gifted or talented | |
|---|---|
| CHARACTERISTICS | SOCIAL SUPPORTS |
| • Often has very strong emotions, interests, and opinions<br>• May be preoccupied with their own thoughts and plans so may not respond to others in appropriate ways<br>• May have difficulty with transitions and want things to go according to their plans<br>• May question rules and behave in challenging ways, especially if feeling frustrated or lacking learning opportunities | • Pair with like-minded students<br>• Increase self-regulation by naming feelings and suggesting ways to manage them, listening actively, and promoting problem-solving<br>• Teach "I can always finish this later"<br>• Provide emotional support, particularly if the student is being accelerated into groups with older students |

*(continued on next page)*

## COGNITIVE/NEUROLOGICAL NEEDS (*continued*)

### Mild intellectual disability (MID)

| CHARACTERISTICS | SOCIAL SUPPORTS |
| --- | --- |
| • May be unable to perceive nonverbal cues in social situations and may be viewed as emotionally immature by their peers<br>• Often exhibit obsessive-compulsive behaviours | • Reinforce positive progress, no matter how small or seemingly insignificant<br>• Be prepared to give frequent reminders about appropriate behaviour<br>• Combine visual prompts with verbal cues<br>• Provide specific instruction of prosocial skills<br>• Model positive prosocial skills<br>• Use peer-tutoring as appropriate<br>• Be patient and maintain your sense of humour |

### Severe intellectual disability (SID)

| CHARACTERISTICS | SOCIAL SUPPORTS |
| --- | --- |
| • Greater limitations than MID in intellectual abilities and adaptive functioning (including personal care, communication, and social skills) | • Model positive interactions and point out strengths to other students<br>• Be alert to bullying<br>• Combine gestures with verbal prompts<br>• Consistently utilize plan for instruction<br>• Use step by step instruction<br>• Use assistive technology<br>• Be patient and maintain your sense of humour<br>• Reinforce positive progress |

### Autism spectrum disorders (ASDs)

| CHARACTERISTICS | SOCIAL SUPPORTS |
| --- | --- |
| • Lacks or has delay in social and communication skills<br>• Depending on the extent of the disorder, may exhibit:<br>› Delays in speech development<br>› Difficulty reading nonverbal cues<br>› Failure to understand others' feelings<br>› Difficulty understanding jokes, sarcasm, or teasing<br>› Difficulty or inability to carry on a conversation<br>› Excessive repetition of words (echolalia)<br>› Unrelated answers to questions | • Provide supportive peer partners<br>• Consider directing teaching and practice with social skills<br>• Be alert to bullying<br>• Model positive prosocial skills<br>• Combine gestures with verbal prompts<br>• Focus on behaviours that support positive social outcomes (friendship, happiness)<br>• Be patient and maintain your sense of humour<br>• Reinforce positive progress |

| Attention deficit disorder (ADD) and attention deficit hyperactivity disorder (ADHD) | |
| --- | --- |
| CHARACTERISTICS | SOCIAL SUPPORTS |
| • Inattention, impulsiveness, and/or hyperactivity may result in negative responses from classmates and adults | • Model respect and patience<br>• Support children with their challenges and encourage them to advocate for themselves<br>• Provide classroom programs to develop positive thinking and social-emotional skills<br>• Directly teach specific strategies<br>• Reinforce positive progress<br>• Use mnemonic strategies |

| Learning disabilities (LDs) | |
| --- | --- |
| RANGE OF CHALLENGES | LEARNING SUPPORTS |
| • May have more difficulty solving social problems, adjusting to the characteristics of their listeners, and dealing with peer pressure<br>• May struggle with giving and accepting criticism and have a lower tolerance for frustration and failure<br>• More likely to be subject to unsupportive comments from adults<br>• Social skills vary | • Teach mindfulness strategies to help students become more aware of themselves and their surroundings<br>• Direct teaching for social interaction skills<br>• Model patience and respect<br>• Support confidence and self esteem<br>• Reinforce positive progress |

## SOCIAL/EMOTIONAL/BEHAVIOURAL NEEDS

| CHARACTERISTICS | SOCIAL SUPPORTS |
| --- | --- |
| • Interacts dysfunctionally with environment (e.g., classroom, home, community)<br>• Challenging behaviours may relate to traumatic experiences | • Try to understand what student is trying to communicate or accomplish with behaviours, then create a plan to make negative behaviour unnecessary<br>• Teach positive problem-solving<br>• Support self-confidence by recognizing strengths and achievements<br>• Reinforce positive progress<br>• Model positive prosocial skills<br>• Anticipate and redirect negative behaviour as you see it starting |

(continued on next page)

## COMMUNICATION, SPEECH, AND LANGUAGE NEEDS

| CHALLENGES | SOCIAL SUPPORTS |
|---|---|
| • Difficulties with speech and/or language can cause students to feel neglected or rejected by peers | • Model for all students by speaking clearly and a bit slower than normal, pausing at appropriate times, and using simple language and grammar<br>• Make eye contact when student is speaking and don't interrupt |

## ENGLISH LANGUAGE LEARNERS

| EXAMPLES | SOCIAL SUPPORTS |
|---|---|
| • Indigenous students who speak an Indigenous language at home<br>• Students who arrive as immigrants from non-English-speaking countries<br>• Students born in Canada to parents who speak limited English | • Model positive prosocial skills<br>• Reinforce positive progress<br>• Provide peer support<br>• Use visual cues and gestures |

## SENSORY NEEDS

### Hearing

| EXAMPLES AND CHARACTERISTICS | SOCIAL SUPPORTS |
|---|---|
| • Hearing needs may be loosely categorized as:<br>  › *Deafness.* Severe to profound deficits in ability to hear. May use American Sign Language (ASL) or amplification devices<br>  › *Mild to moderate hearing loss.* Usually has hearing aids to amplify sounds. Speech and language development often delayed<br>• In mainstream classrooms, may feel lonely and socially isolated | • Work with student to help them advocate for what they need to feel included<br>• Help peers understand how to communicate with student<br>• Make use of technology to facilitate communication<br>• Consider small group activities based on hobbies or interests |

### Vision

| CHARACTERISTICS | SOCIAL SUPPORTS |
|---|---|
| • Social skill learning is inhibited by:<br>  › A lack of information about the visual aspects of interacting with others<br>  › The hesitation of others to initiate contact or communicate appropriate expectations | • Model appropriate social behaviour<br>• Provide opportunities for students to learn and practice prosocial skills<br>• Consider small group activities based on hobbies or interests |

## CHRONIC HEALTH / MEDICAL NEEDS

| EXAMPLES | SOCIAL SUPPORTS |
| --- | --- |
| • May feel isolated from the normal activities and interactions of the classroom due to long or frequent periods of hospitalization<br>• May feel like an outsider | • Use technology to help classmates connect with student and vice versa while student is away<br>• Reinforce positive progress<br>• Provide peer support<br>• Model positive prosocial skills |

# Appendix E

# A Continuum Framework for Responding to Children

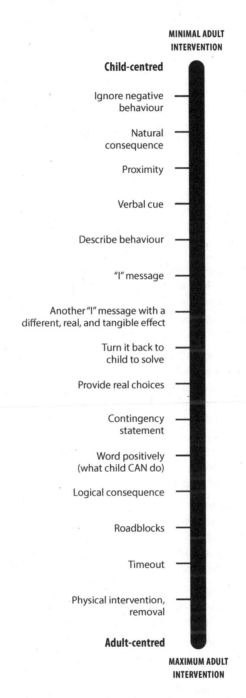

**MINIMAL ADULT
INTERVENTION**

**Child-centred**

Ignore negative
behaviour

Natural
consequence

Proximity

Verbal cue

Describe behaviour

"I" message

Another "I" message with a
different, real, and tangible effect

Turn it back to
child to solve

Provide real choices

Contingency
statement

Word positively
(what child CAN do)

Logical consequence

Roadblocks

Timeout

Physical intervention,
removal

**Adult-centred**

**MAXIMUM ADULT
INTERVENTION**

*Note.* Switch gears to active listening whenever you see that a child is upset (except in cases where physical removal is the only option). Printed with permission from Matheson (2017), who cites Wolfgang and Glickman (1980) and Oken-Wright (1992).

# Glossary

**Accommodations.** Supports and services provided to help a student access information and demonstrate learning.

**Active listening.** A skill that allows an individual to engage with the speaker more effectively by paying special attention to the conversation and focusing on genuinely understanding the speaker rather than on responding. Active listening strategies include attentive listening, asking open-ended questions, and paraphrasing.

**Adaptations.** Changes made to allow students who have exceptionalities to adapt to the learning environment. Curriculum standards remain the same.

**Alternative expectations.** Development of skills that are not represented in the curriculum.

**Aphasia.** A communication disorder in which an individual can hear a message but cannot understand its meaning or produce meaningful sentences. This is caused by brain injury.

**Apraxia.** A neurological condition characterized by an inability to sequence muscle movements and therefore to produce meaningful speech.

**Autism spectrum disorders.** Disorders characterized by varying degrees of difficulty with communication and social interactions. There are sometimes repetitive or restrictive patterns of thought and behaviour.

**Book awareness.** An understanding of the nature and uses of books.

**Differentiating instruction.** Planning instruction according to the needs of individual students.

**Diversity.** The presence of a wide range of human characteristics within a group. The dimensions of diversity include, but are not limited to, ancestry, culture, ethnicity, gender identity, language, physical and intellectual ability, race, religion, sex, sexual orientation, and socioeconomic status.

**Emergent literacy.** A term used to explain a child's knowledge of reading and writing skills before they learn how to read and write words.

**Environment.** The surroundings or conditions in which a person, animal, or plant lives or functions. For example, the environments a student might experience include school, classroom, home, and community.

**Ethnicity.** A social group that has a common national or cultural tradition.

**Exceptionality.** An area of functioning in which a student is significantly different from the average. This includes children with special gifts and talents as well as those with disabilities.

**Expressive language.** The use of words, sentences, gestures, and writing to convey meaning and messages to others.

**Gender identity.** A person's internal sense of being male, female, some combination of male and female, or neither male nor female.

**Guided reading.** A method of reading where the adult works with a small group of students who are grouped according to their reading ability using materials appropriate to their skill level.

**Inclusion.** A process that helps to overcome barriers limiting the presence, participation, and achievement of learners.

**Inclusive education.** Education that is based on the principles of acceptance and inclusion of all students.

**Independent reading level.** The difficulty level of material that a child can comfortably read and comprehend without the support of an adult.

**Individual education plan (IEP).** A written plan/program with input from the teacher, EA, parents/guardians, and other consultants that specifies a student's academic goals and the method to obtain these goals.

**Integration.** A classroom structure in which students with exceptionalities are placed in mainstream education settings with some adaptations and resources, but on condition that they can fit in with preexisting structures, attitudes, and a largely unaltered environment.

**Intergenerational trauma.** The transmission of historical oppression and its negative consequences across generations.

**Levelled reading books.** Reading material that has been coded with a specific level of readability.

**Literacy.** The ability to read, write, and use numbers.

**Literature circle.** A teaching strategy in which students meet in small groups to discuss a book that the group has chosen. Each member of the group is assigned a role in the discussion.

**Modifications.** Changes that are made in what a student is expected to learn. The curriculum is adapted to meet a student's individual needs and students may be assessed using different criteria.

**Multiple intelligences.** Howard Gardner's theory that people learn and acquire information in a variety of different ways that correspond to different types of intelligence. Intelligence, according to this theory, is not a single characteristic; rather, intelligence has many facets. These include intelligence relating to words, numbers, images, music, social interaction, introspection, physical movement, and attunement to nature.

**Nonverbal communication.** The transmission of messages without the use of words (e.g., by gestures, use of space, etc.).

**Number sense.** The ability to understand numbers and use them in flexible ways.

**Numeracy.** The ability to reason and apply simple numerical concepts. Basic numeracy includes understanding foundational skills like addition, subtraction, multiplication, and division.

**Orofacial defects.** Birth defects that affect the upper lip and the roof of the mouth (such as cleft lips and palates) that cause difficulty with speaking and eating.

**Paraphrasing.** Restating a text, passage, or other communication in another form or in other words as a means of clarifying meaning. Active listening could involve paraphrasing either words or nonverbal emotions.

**Partner reading.** A cooperative learning strategy in which two students take turns reading and providing feedback to each other as a way to increase fluency and monitor comprehension.

**Readers' workshop.** An instructional method that combines large amounts of independent reading with whole class and small group discussions (sometimes compared to a book club or a dining room table discussion).

**Print awareness.** The understanding of the basic concepts of print, including that print carries meaning and follows a set of rules.

**Receptive language.** The ability to understand words and language range of human qualities and attributes within a group, organization, or society.

**Roadblocks.** Adult-driven responses that stymie learning and discussion and get in the way of active, open listening.

**Scaffolding.** A process for providing intentional supports during the learning process. It is designed specifically to lead to a deeper level of student learning.

**Secondary traumatic stress (STS).** Stress or trauma symptoms experienced as a result of working with persons who have been traumatized.

**Self-concept.** How we describe and think about ourselves. For example, we may describe ourselves as shy.

**Self-esteem.** How we judge or value ourselves. For example, we may describe ourselves as shy (self-concept) but whether we feel negatively or positively about this characteristic relates to our self-esteem.

**Self-regulation.** The ability to exercise self-control of emotions and behaviours.

**Sexual orientation.** A person's identity in relation to the gender or genders to which they are sexually attracted (e.g., homosexual, heterosexual, bisexual, pansexual, etc.).

**Shared reading.** A teaching strategy in which the adult reads aloud while students follow along.

**Special education.** Classes or instruction designed specifically and exclusively for students categorized as having special educational needs / exceptionalities.

**Sound awareness.** The ability to distinguish and work with sounds.

**Think–pair–share.** A collaborative learning strategy in which students work together to solve a problem or answer a question about an assigned reading or question. It involves three steps: thinking individually, sharing ideas with a partner, then sharing with the larger group.

**Tiered instruction.** A method of instruction that varies the level of assignments such that students are working on the same task but at different levels.

**Trauma.** The psychological effects of severe and/or long-term stress from an event or series of events that are perceived as threats to one's safety or to the stability of one's world.

**Trauma-informed.** The state of recognizing that trauma has many forms, and people have many kinds of trauma in their lives.

**Universal design for learning (UDL).** An educational framework that guides the development of flexible learning environments that can accommodate individual learning differences.

**Word identification skills.** The ability to read words accurately and automatically.

**Zone of proximal development (ZPD).** A concept developed by Lev Vygotsky to describe the difference between what a student can do without help and what they can accomplish with competent assistance.

# Bibliography

Ainscow, M., & Messiou, K. (2018). Engaging with the views of students to promote inclusion in education. *Journal of Educational Change*, 19(1), 1–17. doi: 10.1007/s10833-017-9312-1

Airton, L. (2020). *Gender: Your guide*. Toronto: Simon and Schuster.

Alberta Education. (2019). *Guidelines for time-out in Alberta schools*. Retrieved from Government of Alberta website: https://www.alberta.ca/assets/ documents/ed-guidelines-for-time-out-in-alberta-schools.pdf

Alberta Teachers' Association (ATA). (2016). *Teachers and educational assistants: Roles and responsibilities*. https://www.teachers.ab.ca/SiteCollection Documents/ATA/Publications/Teachers-as-Professionals/MON-5%20 Teachers%20and%20Educational%20Assistants.pdf

AllOntario Team. (2014, April 8). *Achieving excellence: A renewed vision for education in Ontario*. AllOntario. https://allontario.ca/a-renewed-vision-for -education-in-ontario

American Academy of Child and Adolescent Psychiatry (AACAP). (2013, August). *Facts for families* (no. 92). https://www.aacap.org/AACAP/Families _and_Youth/Facts_for_Families/FFF-Guide/Children%20with%20Lesbian, %20Gay-Bisexual-and-Transgender-Parents-92.aspx

August, D. (Ed.). (2006). *Developing literacy in second-language learners: Report of the National Literacy Panel on Language-Minority Children and Youth* (T. Shanahan, Chair). Mahwah, NJ: Lawrence Erlbaum Associates.

Barber, K. (Ed.). (2004). *The Canadian Oxford Dictionary* (2nd ed.). Oxford University Press.

Beedie, N., Macdonald, D., & Wilson, D. (2019, July 9). *Towards justice: Tackling Indigenous child poverty in Canada*. Upstream and Canadian Centre for Policy Alternatives. Retrieved from Child care Canada: Childcare resources and research unit website: https://www.childcarecanada.org/documents/

research-policy-practice/19/07/towards-justice-tackling-indigenous-child
-poverty-canada

Bialystok, E. (2011). Reshaping the mind: The benefits of bilingualism. *Canadian Journal of Experimental Psychology*, 65(4), 229–235. doi: 10.1037/a0025406

Block, S. (2017, October 27). Canada's population is changing but income inequality remains a problem. *Behind the Numbers, Canadian Centre for Policy Alternatives*. http://behindthenumbers.ca/2017/10/27/population -changing-income-inequality-remains/

Brackett, M. (2019, December). *SEL Exchange Webinar Series: From Theory to Practice to Systemic Change, Marc Brackett (Dec 2019)* [Video conference presentation]. YouTube. https://www.youtube.com/watch?v=lkVjflR-21A

Bradfield, T.A., Besner, A.C., Wackerle-Hollman, A.K., Albano, A.D., Rodriguez, M.C., & McConnell, S.R. (2014). Redefining individual growth and development indicators: Oral language. *Assessment for Effective Intervention*, 39(4), 233–244. doi: 10.1177/1534508413496837

Branden, N. (1995). Six pillars of self-esteem. USA: Random House.

British Columbia Teachers' Federation (BCTF). (2010). *Poverty and education: A teacher's perspective: Summary of the findings of the focus group research.* https://bctf.ca/uploadedFiles/Public/Publications/ResearchReports/ 2012-EI-01.pdf

Canadian Mental Health Association (CMHA) Ontario. (n.d.). *Lesbian, gay, bisexual, trans & queer identified people and mental health.* CMHA Ontario. https://ontario.cmha.ca/documents/lesbian-gay-bisexual-trans-queer -identified-people-and-mental-health/

Canadian Multiculturalism Act, Revised Statutes of Canada (1985, c. 24 (4th Supp.) [1988, c. 31]). Retrieved from the Justice Laws website: https://laws -lois.justice.gc.ca/eng/acts/C-18.7/page-1.html

Canadian Teachers' Federation. (2020). *Poverty: Professional knowledge on key issues affecting education.* Canadian Teachers' Federation website. https:// web.archive.org/web/20190608084049/https://www.ctf-fce.ca/en/Pages/ Issues/Poverty.aspx

Canadian Union of Public Employees (CUPE). (n.d.). *Code of ethics: Educational assistants and youth service workers.* http://www.cupe3260.ca/documents/ Code%20of%20Ethics.pdf

Causton-Theoharis, J. (2009) *The paraprofessional's handbook for effective support in inclusive classrooms.* Baltimore: Paul H. Brookes.

Center on the Developing Child, Harvard University. (2020). *Resilience.* Harvard University website. https://developingchild.harvard.edu/science/ key-concepts/resilience/

Center on the Developing Child. (n.d.). *The impact of early adversity on children's development.* Harvard University website. https://developingchild

.harvard.edu/resources/inbrief-the-impact-of-early-adversity-on-childrens
-development

Centers for Disease Control and Prevention (CDC). (2017). *LGBT Youth.* Lesbian, gay, bisexual, and transgender health. https://www.cdc.gov/lgbthealth/youth.html

Cheminais, R. (2010). *Special education needs for newly qualified teachers and teaching assistants* (2nd ed.). London: Routledge.

Chess, S., & Thomas, A. (1996). *Temperament: Theory and practice.* London: Routledge.

Child Welfare Information Gateway. (2014). *Parenting a child who has experienced trauma* [Brochure]. USA: Children's Bureau. Retrieved from Children's Bureau website: https://www.childwelfare.gov/pubPDFs/child-trauma.pdf

Chin, N.B., & Wigglesworth, G. (2007). *Bilingualism: An advanced resource book.* London: Routledge.

Cornell University. (2017). *What does the scholarly research say about the well-being of children with gay or lesbian parents?* What we know: The public policy research portal. https://whatweknow.inequality.cornell.edu/topics/lgbt-equality/what-does-the-scholarly-research-say-about-the-wellbeing-of-children-with-gay-or-lesbian-parents/

Cox, J. (n.d.). *Differentiated instruction strategies: Tiered assignments.* TeachHub. https://www.teachhub.com/differentiated-instruction-strategies-using-tiered-assignments

Daschuk, J. (2013). *Clearing the plains: Disease, politics of starvation, and the loss of Aboriginal life.* Regina: University of Regina Press.

Department of Education and Skills. (2011). *Literacy and Numeracy for Learning and Life: The National Strategy to Improve Literacy and Numeracy Among Children and Young People 2011-2020.* Seomra Ranga. https://www.seomraranga.com/2011/07/literacy-and-numeracy-for-learning-and-life/

Diamond, A. (2016, February 22). *To improve self-regulation, creativity and problem-solving let children play* [Presentation slides]. Retrieved from SlideShare: https://www.slideshare.net/bcmuseum/selfregulation-creativity-and-problemsolving-through-play

Diamond, A. (n.d.). *Leveraging what we've learned from brain research to help every child succeed* [Presentation slides]. Retrieved from ParentMap: http://www.parentmap.com/images/brain_research_to_help_every_child_succeed_-_adele_diamond.pdf

Dixon, S. (2005). Inclusion—not segregation or integration is where a student with special needs belongs. *Journal of Educational Thought*, 39(1), 33–53.

Dweck, C. (2006). *Mindset: The new psychology of success.* New York: Ballantyne.

Fine, S. (2015, May 28). Chief Justice says Canada attempted 'cultural genocide' on aboriginals. *The Globe and Mail.* https://www.theglobeandmail.com/

news/national/chief-justice-says-canada-attempted-cultural-genocide-on
-aboriginals/article24688854/

Fountas, I., & Pinnell, G. (1996). *Guided reading: Good first teaching for all children.* Portsmouth: Heinemann.

Friesen, J., & Bascaramurty, D. (2011, December16). Canadian schools struggle with what to do about Christmas. *The Globe and Mail.* https://www.theglobe andmail.com/life/holiday-guide/canadian-schools-struggle-with-what-to -do-about-christmas/article1357339/

Galer, D. (2015). Disability rights movement in Canada. In B. Graves (Ed.), *The Canadian encyclopedia.* https://www.thecanadianencyclopedia.ca/en/article/ disability-rights-movement

Gardener, H. (1993). *Frames of mind: A theory of multiple intelligences.* New York: Basic Books.

Gebhard, A. (2018). 'Let's make a little drum': Limitations and contradictory effects of cultural approaches in Indigenous education, *Race, Ethnicity and Education,* 21(6), 757–772. doi: 10.1080/13613324.2017.1377172

Genesee, F., & Lindholm-Leary, K. (2011). The education of English language learners. In K. Harris, S. Graham, & T. Urdan (Eds.), *APA Educational Psychology Handbook* (Vol. 3, 499–526). Washington, DC: APA Books.

Government of Alberta. (n.d.). *Inclusive education.* Government of Alberta website. https://www.alberta.ca/inclusive-education.aspx

Government of Alberta. (n.d.). *What is child abuse, neglect and sexual exploitation: Find out how to know and recognize the warning signs.* Government of Alberta website. https://www.alberta.ca/what-is-child-abuse-neglect-and -sexual-exploitation.aspx

Government of Canada. (2017, February 10). *Backgrounder on poverty in Canada.* Government of Canada website. https://www.canada.ca/en/ employment-social-development/programs/poverty-reduction/ backgrounder.html

Government of Canada. (2017, November 14). *Rights of children.* Government of Canada website. https://www.canada.ca/en/canadian-heritage/services/ rights-children.html

Government of Canada. (2019, July 25). *Social and economic influences on health.* Government of Canada website. https://www.canada.ca/en/ public-health/services/health-promotion/population-health/what -determines-health.html

Government of Ontario. (2017). *Ontario's education equity action plan.* https:// ocsta.on.ca/ocsta/wp-content/uploads/2013/04/8-Equity-Action-Plan _AODA_FINAL.pdf

Government of Ontario. (2009). *Ontario's equity and inclusive education strategy.* http://www.edu.gov.on.ca/eng/policyfunding/equity.pdf

Hackett, C., Feeny, D., & Tompa, P. (2016). Canada's residential school system: Measuring the intergenerational impact of familial attendance on health and mental health outcomes. *Journal of Epidemiology and Community Health, 70,* 1096–1105. doi: 10.1136/jech-2016-207380

Harber, M., & Rao, A. (Eds.). (2019). *The role of an education assistant: Supporting inclusion.* Toronto: Canadian Scholars.

Holdgreve-Resendez, R. (2010, October 13). *Concepts of print and genre.* Legit Literacy. https://legitliteracy.weebly.com/concepts-of-print.html

Hutchinson, N., & Specht, J. (2020). *Inclusion of learners with exceptionalities in Canadian schools* (6th ed.). North York: Pearson.

Hyatt, C., Sleep, C., Lamkin, J., Maples-Keller, J., Sedikides, C., & Miller, J. (2018). Narcissism and self-esteem: A nomological network analysis. *Plos One,* 1 August 2018. https://doi.org/10.1371/journal.pone.0201088

Inclusion BC. (n.d.). *What is inclusive education?* https://inclusionbc.org/our -resources/what-is-inclusive-education/

Inclusive Education Canada. (n.d.). *What is inclusive education?* https://inclusive education.ca/about/what-is-ie/

James, W. (1890/1983). *The principles of psychology.* Cambridge, MA: Harvard University Press.

Jesuit Social Services. (2009). *Working cross culturally: Refugees - trauma, grief and loss.* Strong Bonds. http://www.strongbonds.jss.org.au/workers/cultures/ refugees.html

Jones, C.D., Clark, S.K., & Reutzel, D.R. (2013). Enhancing alphabet knowledge instruction: Research implications and practical strategies for early childhood educators. *Early Childhood Education Journal,* 41(1), 81–89. doi: 10.1007/ s10643-012-0534-9

Kagan, J. (2019). Temperament (Rev. 2nd ed.). In R. Tremblay, M. Boivin & R.D. Peters (Eds.), *Encyclopedia of early childhood development.* http://www .child-encyclopedia.com/temperament/according-experts/temperament

Kahn, J. (2013, September 11). Can emotional intelligence be taught? *The New York Times Magazine.* https://www.nytimes.com/2013/09/15/magazine/ can-emotional-intelligence-be-taught.html

Kaiser, B. (2020, March 25). *Understanding the impact of trauma on behaviour* [Webinar recording]. Early Childhood Investigations Webinars. https://www .earlychildhoodwebinars.com/webinars/understanding-the-impact-of -trauma-on-behavior-by-barbara-kaiser/

Katz, J. (2012). *Teaching to diversity: The three-block model of universal design for learning.* Winnipeg: Portage and Main Press.

Kaufman, S.B. (2017, October 29). Narcissism and self-esteem are very different. *Beautiful minds: Scientific American.* https://blogs.scientificamerican.com/ beautiful-minds/narcissism-and-self-esteem-are-very-different/

Kemble, T. (2019, October). *Indigenous early learning and care in the City of Edmonton: Articulating the experiences, perspectives and needs of Indigenous parents/caregivers.* A report prepared for the Edmonton Council for Early Learning and Care.

Keung, N. (2019, July 9). Almost half of Status First Nations children live in poverty, study finds. *The Star.* https://www.thestar.com/news/gta/2019/07/09/almost-half-of-status-first-nations-children-live-in-poverty-study-finds.html

Kipfer, A. (2015). *Education assistants supporting inclusive education in secondary schools* (Master's thesis). Retrieved from Western University Electronic Thesis and Dissertation Repository: https://ir.lib.uwo.ca/etd/3363

Kirup, K. (2018, November 12). Indigenous women coerced into sterilizations across Canada: senator. *CBC News.* https://www.cbc.ca/news/politics/sterilization-indigenous-1.4902303

Kovacs, A., & Mehler, J. (2009). Flexible learning of multiple speech structures in bilingual infants. *Science, 325*(5940), 611–12. doi: 10.1126/science.1173947

Leu, D. (2000). Our children's future: Changing the focus of literacy and literacy instruction. *The Reading Teacher, 53*(5), 424–428.

Lynch, M. (2018, November 21). Assistive technology for students with disabilities. *The Tech Edvocate.* https://www.thetechedvocate.org/assistive-technology-students-disabilities/

MacDonald, D., & Wilson, D. (2013). *Poverty or prosperity: Indigenous children in Canada.* Canadian Centre for Policy Alternatives. https://www.policyalternatives.ca/sites/default/files/uploads/publications/National%20Office/2013/06/Poverty_or_Prosperity_Indigenous_Children.pdf

Marsh, J. (2011, November 30). Eugenics: Keeping Canada sane. *Jamesmarsh.com.* http://www.jameshmarsh.com/2011/11/eugenics-keeping-canada-sane/

Martschenko, D. (2018, February 1). The IQ test wars: Why screening for intelligence is still so controversial. *The Conversation.* http://theconversation.com/the-iq-test-wars-why-screening-for-intelligence-is-still-so-controversial-81428

Maslow, A.H. (1954). *Motivation and personality.* New York: Harper and Row.

Matheson, M.L. (2017). The continuum framework for responding to children: Teacher classified concerns. Unpublished resource.

Mayo Clinic. (2019, April 5). *Stress relief from laughter? It's no joke.* Mayo Clinic website. https://www.mayoclinic.org/healthy-lifestyle/stress-management/in-depth/stress-relief/art-20044456

McCue, H. (2018). Education of Indigenous Peoples in Canada. In B. Graves (Ed.), *The Canadian encyclopedia.* https://www.thecanadianencyclopedia.ca/en/article/aboriginal-people-education

Mehrabian, A. (1972/2017). *Nonverbal communication*. New York: Routledge.

Merritt, J. (2018, March). The Saintly legacy of Fred Rogers. *Winter Park Magazine,* Spring 2018, 70–74. https://winterparkmag.com/2018/03/30/saintly-legacy-fred-rogers/

Mitchell, D. (2015). *Education that fits: Review of international trends in the education of students with special educational needs* (2nd ed.). Christchurch, New Zealand: University of Canterbury.

Mitchell, D. (2014). *What really works in special and inclusive education: Using evidence-based teaching strategies*. London: Routledge.

Moore, S. (n. d.). *Inclusive education: Who, what, where, when, why?!* [Presentation slides]. Retrieved from Blogsomemoore: https://blogsomemoore.files.wordpress.com/2018/03/getca-2.pdf

Morency, J.D., Malenfont, E.C., & MacIsaac, S. (2017). *Immigration and diversity: Population projections for Canada and its regions, 2011 to 2036*. Statistics Canada. https://www150.statcan.gc.ca/n1/pub/91-551-x/91-551-x2017001-eng.htm

National Council for Curriculum and Assessment. (2012). *Literacy in early childhood and primary education (3-8 years)* (Report no. 15). Dublin : NCCA. https://ncca.ie/media/2137/literacy_in_early_childhood_and_primary_education_3-8_years.pdf

Oken-Wright, P. (1992). From tug of war to "let's make a deal": The teacher's role. *Young Children*, 48(1), 15–20.

Ontario Ministry of Children, Community and Social Services. (n.d.). *The eugenics movement and attitudes toward people with disabilities*. OMCCS website. https://www.mcss.gov.on.ca/en/dshistory/reasons/eugenics.aspx

Ontario Network of International Professionals. (2020). *Educational assistant: Occupational profile*. ONIP website. http://www.onip.ca/educational-assistant/

Parekh, G. (2013). *A case for inclusive education*. Toronto District School Board. https://www.tdsb.on.ca/portals/0/aboutus/research/acaseforinclusiveeducation.pdf

Parekh, G. (2018, March 16). *Exploring inclusion in Ontario* (National inclusion education month commentary no. 24). Inclusive Education Canada. https://inclusiveeducation.ca/2018/03/16/exploring-inclusion-in-ontario/

Park, L., & Crocker, J. (2013). Pursuing self-esteem: Implications for self-regulation and relationships. In V. Zeigler-Hill (Ed.), *Self-Esteem*. New York: Psychology Press.

Perry, B. (2014, December). *Social and emotional development in early childhood* [Video]. Presentation at the Chicago Humanities Festival. Retrieved from YouTube: https://www.youtube.com/watch?v=vkJwFRAwDNE

Pfitzer, S. (Host). (2020, January 10). Brain architecture: Laying the foundation (No. 1) [Audio podcast episode]. In *Brain Architects*. Center on the Developing

Child, Harvard University. https://developingchild.harvard.edu/resources/
the-brain-architects-podcast-brain-architecture-laying-the-foundation/

Pickens, I.B., & Tschopp, N. (2017). *Trauma-informed classrooms*. National Council of Juvenile and Family Court Judges. https://www.ncjfcj.org/wp-content/
uploads/2017/10/NCJFCJ_SJP_Trauma_Informed_Classrooms_Final.pdf

Poole, N., Talbot, C., & Nathoo, T. (2017). *Healing families, helping systems: A
trauma informed practice guide for working with children, youth and families*.
BC Ministry of Children and Family Development. https://www2.gov.bc.ca/
assets/gov/health/child-teen-mental-health/trauma-informed_practice
_guide.pdf

Qvortrup, A., & Qvortrup, L. (2018). Inclusion: Dimensions of inclusion in
education. *International Journal of Inclusive Education*, 22(7), 803–817. doi:
10.1080/13603116.2017.1412506

Robert, A.M., & Gilkinson, T. (2012). *Mental health and well-being of recent
immigrants in Canada: Evidence from the Longitudinal Survey of Immigrants to
Canada (LSIC)* (Ref. no. RR20130301). Government of Canada. https://www
.canada.ca/content/dam/ircc/migration/ircc/english/pdf/research-stats/
mental-health.pdf

Rogers, C. (1959). A theory of therapy, personality and interpersonal relationships as developed in the client-centered framework. In S. Koch (Ed.), *Psychology: A study of a science* (Vol. 3). New York: McGraw Hill.

Rogers, F. (Creator). (1968). *Mister Rogers' Neighborhood* [Television series].
Pittsburgh, PA: WQED Studios.

Rogers, F. (2003). *The world according to Mister Rogers: Important things to
remember*. New York: Hachette.

Sapienza, J., & Masten, A.S. (2011). Understanding and promoting resilience
in children and youth. *Current Opinion in Psychiatry*, 24(4), 267–273. doi:
10.1097/YCO.0b013e32834776a8

Sharma, S., & Zbacnik, A. (2020). *Educators for diverse classrooms: A case study
approach to equity and inclusion*. Lanham, MD: Rowman and Littlefield.

Simmons, H. (1982). *From asylum to welfare*. Downsview, ON: National Institute
on Mental Retardation.

Solomon, R. (2009, August 5). Think-pair-share (Lyman, 1981): An equity
pedagogical best practice to increase and vary student participation in
the classroom. *Classroom 2.0*. https://classroom20.com/profiles/blogs/
thinkpairshare-lyman-1981-an

Stagg-Peterson, S., Huston, L., & Loon, R. (2019). Professional lives and initial
teacher education experiences of Indigenous early childhood educators,
childcare workers and teachers in Northern Ontario. *Brock Education*, 28(2),
17–22. doi: 10.26522/BROCKED.V28I2.683

Statistics Canada. (2013). *2011 National household survey: Immigration, place
of birth, citizenship, ethnic origin, visible minorities, language and religion*.

https://www150.statcan.gc.ca/n1/daily-quotidien/130508/dq130508b-info
-eng.htm

Statistics Canada. (2017a). *An increasingly diverse linguistic profile: Corrected data from the 2016 Census.* https://www150.statcan.gc.ca/n1/daily -quotidien/170817/dq170817a-eng.htm?indid=17282-2&indgeo=0

Statistics Canada. (2017b). *Same-sex couples in Canada in 2016.* https://www12 .statcan.gc.ca/census-recensement/2016/as-sa/98-200-x/2016007/98-200 -x2016007-eng.cfm

Stonechild, B. (2006). Aboriginal people of Saskatchewan. In B. Stonechild (Aboriginal Ed.), *The Encyclopedia of Saskatchewan.* https://esask.uregina.ca/ entry/aboriginal_peoplesof_saskatchewan.jsp

Takaloo, N.M., & Ahmade, M.R. (2017). The effect of learners' motivation on their reading comprehension skill: A literature review. *International Journal of Research in English Education,* 2(3), 10–21. doi: 10.18869/acadpub.ijree.2.3.10

Taylor, C.S. (2014, February 22). If we can't say 'Merry Christmas' in Canada, multiculturalism failed. *Huffington Post.* https://www.huffingtonpost.ca/ christopher-stuart-taylor/saying-merry-christmas_b_4490555.html

Tomlinson, C.A. (2000). *Differentiation of instruction in the elementary grades.* ERIC Clearinghouse on Elementary and Early Childhood Education. https:// files.eric.ed.gov/fulltext/ED443572.pdf

Tompkins, G., Bright R., & Winsor P. (2018). *Language and literacy: Content and teaching strategies.* Pearson Canada.

Tuttle, M. (2019). *Forced or coerced sterilization of Indigenous women.* Alberta Civil Liberties Research Centre. http://www.aclrc.com/blog/2019/3/26/ forced-or-coerced-sterilization-of-indigenous-women

UNESCO. (2005). *Guidelines for inclusion: Ensuring access to education for all.* http://www.ibe.unesco.org/sites/default/files/Guidelines_for_Inclusion _UNESCO_2006.pdf

Unger, M., Russell, P., & Connelly, G. (2014). School-based interventions to enhance the resilience of students. *Journal of Educational and Developmental Psychology,* 4(1), 66–83. doi: 10.5539/jedp.v4n1p66

USA National Early Literacy Panel. (2008). *Developing early literacy: Report of the National Early Literacy Panel.* Washington DC: National Institute for Literacy. https://lincs.ed.gov/publications/pdf/NELPReport09.pdf

Vygotsky, L. (1978). *Mind in society: The development of higher psychological processes.* US: The President and Fellows of Harvard College.

Wasykowski, J. (2001). Perspectives of teacher assistants working with students with diverse learning needs [Master's thesis]. Retrieved from OPUS, University of Lethbridge Research Repository: https://opus.uleth.ca/ bitstream/handle/10133/152/MQ68350.pdf;jsessionid=C87EF9D1A3CF0787 977EAC27681A669D?sequence=3

Wolfensberger, W., Nirje, B., Olansky, S., Perske, R., & Roos, P. (1972). *The principle of normalization in human services.* Downsview, ON: Canadian National Institute on Mental Retardation. Retrieved from University of Nebraska Medical Centre Digital Commons: https://digitalcommons.unmc.edu/cgi/view content.cgi?article=1000&context=wolf_books

Wolfgang, C., & Glickman, C. (1980). *Solving discipline problems: Strategies for classroom teachers.* Boston: Allyn & Bacon, Inc.

Zeigler-Hill, V. (2013). *Self-esteem.* New York: Psychology Press.

# About the Authors

**Carole Massing** began her career as an elementary school teacher and developed a special interest in early learning when her own children were small. Since that time, she has taught in post-secondary programs at MacEwan University, the University of Alberta, and NorQuest College. She has also consulted, researched, and developed curriculum in early learning and child care, interculturalism, and human service administration. Carole teaches in the Bachelor of Applied Human Service Administration program at MacEwan University. She earned her PhD in elementary education at the University of Alberta.

**Bonnie Anderson** began her teaching career as an educational assistant and went on to work as a classroom teacher for three decades. She worked primarily with children with exceptionalities in inclusive and specialized programs. Bonnie developed and coordinated a very successful arts-based program at her school. Her focus was integrating arts across the curriculum and differentiating instruction. She now teaches at NorQuest College in the Educational Assistant program and the Early Learning and Child Care program, and has just developed the curriculum for a new program for EAs.

**Carol Anderson** is a retired educator with 39 years of teaching experience working with school-aged children in diverse classroom settings. She is trained both as a K–12 educator and as a specialist for children with communicative challenges, in particular children who are Deaf and hard of hearing. She brings expertise in working with children who have a wide range of exceptionalities, creating positive, inclusive classrooms, and differentiating instruction for all learners. Originally from California, Carol completed her undergraduate degree in liberal arts from the University of the Pacific and achieved her Master's in Communicative Disorders: Education of the Deaf, at California State University, Fresno.